Critical Guides to Spanish Texts

Critical Guides to Spanish Texts

EDITED BY J. E. VAREY AND A. D. DEYERMOND

PÉREZ GALDÓS

Fortunata y Jacinta

Geoffrey Ribbans

Gilmour Professor
University of Liverpool

Grant & Cutler Ltd *in association with*
Tamesis Books Ltd 1977

© Grant & Cutler Ltd
1977

ISBN 0 7293 0041 2

I.S.B.N. 84-399-7799-9

DEPÓSITO LEGAL: V. 3.308 - 1977

Printed in Spain by
Artes Gráficas Soler, S.A., Valencia
for
GRANT & CUTLER LTD
11 BUCKINGHAM STREET, LONDON, W.C.2

Contents

Prefatory Note

No available edition is wholly reliable. The edition I have used, and to which page references are given, is Benito Pérez Galdós, *Obras completas*, ed. F.C. Sainz de Robles, vol. V (Madrid: Aguilar, 3rd ed. 1961), pp. 13-548. There are also single-volume editions of the novel by Hernando (Madrid), Austral (Buenos Aires), and Porrúa (Mexico City). To facilitate references to these editions and to other Aguilar editions with varying pagination, I have frequently indicated Part, Chapter and Section as follows: III, vii, 5; the page number, when also noted, comes in fourth position. The figures in parenthesis in italic type refer to the numbered items in the Bibliographical Note; where necessary they are followed by page numbers.

No critical edition taking into account the versions of the novel in manuscript or galley proof has yet appeared. Without making any attempt at completeness, I have on occasion drawn on these resources in this study. I have pleasure in acknowledging the generous assistance of the Leverhulme Trust in granting me a research award in 1975-1976 to enable me to consult these texts at Harvard and Las Palmas. My sincere thanks are due to Mr H. B. Hall who has made valuable observations on the manuscript, to Mr A. G. Hodgkiss, Senior Cartographer of the Department of Geography, University of Liverpool, and his staff for the meticulous preparation of the maps and to Mrs Rosemary Morris for her attentive and careful typing of the text through its many revisions.

The English translation by Lester Clarke (Penguin Classics, 1973) is marred by mistranslations, but the translations into French, by Robert Marrast (Lausanne, 1970, 3 vols) and into German, by Kurt Kuhn (Zurich, 1961) can be recommended.

I Introduction

The rise of the realist novel in Spain is customarily attributed to the intellectual ferment produced by the Glorious Revolution of September 1868 which overthrew Queen Isabella II;[1] and if the *Gloriosa* provided the incentive, the stability gained with the Restoration of Isabella's son Alfonso XII in December 1874 made consolidation possible. Certainly the events of this turbulent but stimulating period, which coincides with the years of Galdós's early maturity —he was 25 in 1868 and 32 in 1875— influenced him profoundly and it is significant that these years form the background against which the action of many of his novels, including *Fortunata y Jacinta*, takes place.

The first products of this new impulse appear in the 1870s, but the full flowering comes in the eighties when the majority of the key works of Pereda and Pardo Bazán were written. *Fortunata y Jacinta* (four volumes, 1886-7) dates from this decade, as does Leopoldo Alas's *La Regenta*, *Fortunata*'s only rival, in scope, quality and length,[2] which had appeared two years earlier in 1884 and 1885.

Likewise, *Fortunata* comes at the full maturing of Galdós's own talents when he was in his early forties. His fourteenth novel (excluding the historically-oriented *episodios nacionales*) and the seventh of his fully-fledged *novelas contemporáneas* inaugurated with *La desheredada* (1881), it occupies a central position in his production. He was to continue to write prolifically and at a very high level (thirteen further novels, culminating in *Misericordia*, 1897) for a further decade.

There is no space, within the scope of this guide, to present an adequate discussion of Realism or the realist novel. For the purposes of this study, however, we may adopt the working definition of realism by René Wellek: 'the objective representation of contemporary

---

[1] See Clarín's 'El libre examen y nuestra literatura presente', reproduced and commented on in Sergio Beser, *Leopoldo Alas: teoría y crítica de la novela española* (Barcelona, 1972), pp. 39-46. Also Juan López Morillas, 'La revolución de Septiembre y la novela española', *Revista de Occidente*, 2ª época, LXVII (1968), 94-114. The 1868 revolution forms the background of *La de Bringas*.

[2] See *Critical Guides to Spanish Texts*, 9, by John Rutherford (London, 1974).

social reality'.[3]

One of Galdós's few critical writings on the novel dates from 1870, at the very outset of his career as a novelist. Its programmatic importance is therefore considerable, as Montesinos has pointed out (*16*, I, pp. 27-35). In these *Observaciones sobre el estado de la novela en España* he asserts that the appropriate subject for the modern novel is 'la clase media, la más olvidada por nuestros novelistas', because it supplies the dynamism for society:

> Esa clase es la que determina el movimiento político, la que administra, la que enseña, la que discute, la que da al mundo los grandes innovadores y los grandes libertinos, los ambiciosos de genio y las ridículas vanidades: ella determina el movimiento comercial, una de las grandes manifestaciones de nuestro siglo, y la que posee la clave de los intereses, elemento poderoso de la vida actual, que da origen en las relaciones humanas a tantos dramas y tan raras peripecias. En la vida exterior se muestra con estos caracteres marcadísimos, por ser ella el alma de la política y el comercio, elementos de progreso, que no por serlo en sumo grado han dejado de fomentar dos grandes vicios en la sociedad, la ambición desmedida y el positivismo. Al mismo tiempo, en la vida doméstica, ¡qué vasto cuadro ofrece esta clase, constantemente preocupada por la organización de la familia! Descuella en primer lugar el problema religioso, que perturba los hogares y ofrece contradicciones que asustan . . . Al mismo tiempo, se observan con pavor los estragos del vicio esencialmente desorganizador de la familia, el adulterio, y se duda si esto ha de ser remediado por la solución religiosa, la moral pura o simplemente por una reforma civil . . . (*4*, p. 324).

Such a vigorous and prophetic manifesto is evidently relevant to all the *novelas contemporáneas* which are to come after, for if the special orientation given to the religious problem anticipates *las novelas de la primera época* such as *Doña Perfecta*, *Gloria* or *La familia de León Roch*, the concern with politics and commerce, ambition and vanity, marriage and adultery fits the subject-matter of the later novels admirably. And it fits *Fortunata*, the longest and most ambitious of them, better than most.

[3]René Wellek, 'The Concept of Realism in Literary Scholarship', in *Concepts of Criticism* (New Haven, 1963), pp. 240-1. It should be noted that Wellek himself indicates the limitations of this description in the course of his article. See also J. P. Stern, *On Realism* (London, 1973): 'The riches of the represented world; its weightiness and resistance to ideals; its consequential logic and circumstantiality —these I take to be among the attributes one would expect to find in realistic literature' (p. 28).

Why, we may ask before proceeding further, did Galdós undertake the writing of such a very extensive, four-tier novel? We know that he had doubts about the reception of a novel of such length (6, p. 220) and it is noteworthy that he abridged it considerably in galley proof. Moreover, he was very anxious that the four parts should be available in quick succession, so that the full impact of the work as a whole should be experienced (7, p. 90). Given these doubts, what made him embark on such a hazardous undertaking?

First, I suggest, he was influenced by a certain dissatisfaction with his previous attempts to run major characters and themes on from one independent novel to another. In this connexion the earlier trilogy *El doctor Centeno* (1883), *Tormento* (1884) and *La de Bringas* (1884) is pertinent. The characters flow on from one novel to another, but remain in a curiously indeterminate state until their time comes for individual development. Thus the first of the series, *El doctor Centeno*, is distinctly bitty, for it puts into motion three full stories, those of Pepe Centeno and of the priest Polo, as well as that of the aspiring dramatist Alejandro Miquis; only the last is brought to completion in its pages with his death. *Tormento* and *La de Bringas* are much better novels, but perhaps suffer from a measure of narrative experimentation and from having to depend on the previous work for the formative stage of their main characters. In *Fortunata y Jacinta*, by contrast, Galdós has established a structure which is both diverse and unified.

Another reason for the length of the novel must lie in his desire to present a sweeping panorama of near-contemporary life. It is quite clear that he proposes to enclose within the framework of the novel a wide perspective of social life, and in certain respects the coverage is very extensive. Yet it is important not to exaggerate the completeness of the view.

On this count, it is instructive to see what Galdós had to say about the urban proletariat in 1870:

En el pueblo urbano, muy modificado ya por la influencia de la clase media, sobre todo en las grandes ciudades, la dificultad es mayor. Los nuevos elementos ingeridos en la sociedad por las reformas políticas, la pasmosa propagación de ciertas ideas que van penetrando en la últimas jerarquías, la facilidad con que un pueblo dócil y de vivísima imaginación como el nuestro acepta ciertas costumbres, hacen que sea más difícil y complicada la tarea de retratarlo. El pueblo de Madrid es hoy muy poco conocido: se le estudia poco, y sin duda el que quisiera expresarlo con fidelidad y gracia, hallaría enormes inconvenientes y necesitaría un estudio directo y al natural, sumamente enojoso. (*4*, p. 322)

In *Fortunata* Galdós goes a certain way towards attempting this difficult task, especially in reflecting language and the assimilation, real or aspiring, of the *pueblo* into the middle class, but if his aim was anything approaching complete coverage of society, what we are offered is a quite inadequate representation of the mass of the population. But of course it was not; indeed it could not be, whatever the extension of the work. Even within the very ample range Galdós has allowed himself, he has had to select and limit himself to certain areas:[4] aspects, in fact, of two contrasting yet complementary middle-class societies, with a working-class girl caught between them.

As false as the misleading idea of comprehensiveness is the notion of the novel as a neutral representation of life. The emphasis placed on observation and portrayal of society makes for an identification of fiction and life, which is understandable but simplistic. In this respect Stendhal's famous definition 'un roman est un miroir qui se promène sur une grande route' ('the novel is a mirror walking along a highway', *Le Rouge et le Noir*, II, xix) is misleading. The concept is also reinforced by Naturalist theories, and is in fact enunciated by Galdós himself in 1897 in his Academy speech, *La sociedad contemporánea como materia novelable*:

Imagen de la vida es la novela y el arte de componerla estriba en reproducir los caracteres humanos, las pasiones, las debilidades, lo grande y lo pequeño, las almas y las fisonomías, todo lo espiritual y lo físico que nos constituye y nos rodea y el lenguaje que es la marca de la raza, y las viviendas que son el signo de la familia, y la vestidura que diseña los últimos trazos externos de la personalidad: todo esto sin olvidar que debe existir perfecto fiel de balanza entre la exactitud y la belleza de la reproducción.[5]

[4]Compare such comments as Henry James's 'Life being all inclusion and confusion, and art being all discrimination and selection . . .' (p. 75); Flaubert's 'reality, in my view, ought to be no more than a spring-board' (p. 69); and Hardy's 'realism . . . an artificiality distilled from the fruits of closest observation' (p. 74). All quoted in Miriam Allott, *Novelists on the Novel* (London: Routledge Paperback, 1965).

[5]Menéndez y Pelayo – Pereda – Pérez Galdós, *Discursos leídos ante la Real Academia Española* (7 y 21 de febrero de 1897) (Madrid, 1897), pp. 11-12.

This rather conventional statement stresses the undoubted importance of detailed circumstances and contains one or two interesting features like the precedence given to 'lo espiritual' over 'lo físico' and the importance of language, but it is inadequate as a definition of narrative technique, whether realistic or not. The criterion of 'imagen de la vida' takes too little account of the essential difference, so much emphasized by practising novelists and by modern criticism of fiction, between living and the inevitable process of selection and organization involved in writing (see *12*, pp. 141-3). More thorough-going definitions such as the once famous Naturalistic formula of Arne Holz, art = nature − x, in which x = technical limitations of the medium adopted, or Zola's description of Flaubert's *Education sentimentale* as 'a verbal report dictated by the facts' now seem woefully deficient.[6] Much more acceptable is the stress laid on the importance of keen observation. Examples of Galdós's visual alertness abound. The description of the undistinguished and conventional interior of the Santa Cruz residence ('lo que allí se veía no chocaba por original ni tampoco por rutinario') (I, vi, 3); the slums of Mira el Río teeming with children (I, ix, 1-2); Doña Lupe's study dominated by the portrait of her late husband (II, i, 9); the crowded café de Zaragoza when Feijoo seeks out Juan Pablo (III, iv, 8); the hectic preparations supervised by Guillermina for the Viaticum to be received at Mauricia's bedside (III, vi, 2-3); the statue of Philip III in the Plaza Mayor covered in snow, 'con pelliza de armiño y gorro de dormir' (IV, iv, 2): these are only a few characteristic instances.

Another side of the novel's history is emphasized in Galdós's prologue to *La Regenta* written in 1901: 'el humorismo que es quizás la forma más genial de nuestra raza'. Galdós sees the trajectory of the novel as passing from Spain to France and England and advocates a return to Spanish *socarronería* and Cervantes. 'Nuestro arte de la naturalidad —he declares— con su feliz concierto entre lo serio y lo cómico, responde mejor que el francés a la verdad humana'.[7] Humour, especially of this sly ironic sort called *socarronería*, is, as

[6]See F. W. J. Hemmings,*8*, p. 364, and Lilian R. Furst and Peter N. Skrine, *Naturalism* (The Critical Idiom, 18, London, 1971), pp. 70-2.

[7]Leopoldo Alas (Clarín), *La Regenta* (Buenos Aires, 1946), Prólogo, p. 14.

Michael Nimetz demonstrates (*17*) and we shall have occasion to see, fundamental to Galdós's technique.

Elsewhere also Galdós shows himself well aware of the problems of transforming life into art, and it is curious that at the end of *Fortunata y Jacinta*, at Fortunata's funeral, he gives expression to two opposing attitudes to the subject, without overtly choosing between them:

> En el largo trayecto de la Cava al cementerio, que era uno de los del Sur, Segismundo contó al buen Ponce todo lo que sabía de la historia de Fortunata, que no era poco, sin omitir lo último, que era, sin duda, lo mejor; a lo que dijo el eximio sentenciador de obras literarias que había allí elementos para un drama o novela, aunque, a su parecer, el tejido artístico no resultaría vistoso sino introduciendo ciertas urdimbres de todo punto necesarias para que la vulgaridad de la vida pudiese convertirse en materia estética. No toleraba él que la vida se llevase al arte tal como es, sino aderazada, sazonada con olorosas especias y después puesta al fuego hasta que cueza bien. Segismundo no participaba de tal opinión, y estuvieron discutiendo sobre esto con selectas razones de una y otra parte; quedándose cada cual con sus ideas y su convicción, y resultando al fin que la fruta cruda bien madura es cosa muy buena, y que también lo son las compotas, si el repostero sabe lo que trae entre manos. (IV, vi, 16, p. 544)

Unadorned reality ('la vida . . . tal como es', 'la fruta cruda bien madura') or artistic elaboration ('aderazada, sazonada con olorosas especias y después puesta al fuego hasta que cueza bien', 'compotas')? Galdós, typically, does not opt unequivocally for either procedure. On the one hand, he seems to play down the rather facile idea of a straight transposition of life, though the flavour of the ripe fruit should be retained. Moreover, the process of elaboration, he suggests, needs skilled handling. On the other hand, to add to the ambiguity, the critic Ponce, as seen by the terms he employs ('vulgaridad de la vida', 'aderazada, sazonada con olorosas especias') is clearly not the man to undertake the task.

One of the dangers he is most conscious of is that of falling into the fundamental defects of the melodramatic novel, associated with the *novela por entregas* which he had denounced so vigorously in 1870, by exaggerating the emotional impact of events. The temptation is a very real one against which Galdós felt he had to be on his guard. He gets it out of his system by allowing some of his characters to succumb, or to toy with the idea of succumbing, to histrionics. Among the protagonists of his novels the best example of an exaltedly dramatic approach is Alejandro Miquis in *El doctor Centeno*, but Galdós also creates early in his career a most serviceable figure who actually becomes a writer of *folletines* or sensational novels: José Ido del Sagrario, and parodies his work in *Tormento* (*22*). Although this aspect of Ido is not particularly prominent in *Fortunata y Jacinta*, his madness takes its subject from sensationalist novels, and moreover he is very much involved in one of the potentially most melodramatic episodes —that of *el Pitusín*, the abandoned child romantically reclaimed. Juanito, too, is apt to treat his relations with his wife and mistress in a high-flown theatrical tone (I, v, 5, p. 59; III, ii, 1, p. 311; III, vii, 5, p. 414) in order to lift them up from the mean and selfish reality of his conduct. At other times, as we shall see (pp. 52-4 below), the narrative is ironically imbued with heroic rhetoric reflecting the attitude of the characters. People in everyday life, Galdós seems to be saying, are liable to dramatize and exaggerate their emotions; the novel should reflect this aspect of their existence by drawing on the example of the *folletín*, just as Cervantes drew on the romances of chivalry, and at the same time maintain a certain ironic detachment.

No less dangerous than the identification of life and art is the simplistic view that 'characters drawn from life' are different in kind from other fictional characters. The process by which a novelist arrives at a formulation of his characters is always interesting, and to that extent it is relevant to know that several characters from our novel have been copied in some degree from real people. Berkowitz claims that Fortunata herself was one of these (*6*, p. 105); the Viaticum episode involving Mauricia was also based on a real event (p. 107). The clearest example is related to this episode, for Doña Guillermina Pacheco was modelled on a real-life charitable lady, Doña Ernestina Manuel de Villena. More important, though, is the use to which the living model is put. The clear reflection of Doña Ernestina and the use of a real occurrence like Mauricia's death-scene documented by Lucille Braun (*43*) explain nothing at all about such things as the crucial part Doña Guillermina plays in the lives of both Jacinta and Fortunata. To take another case in more detail. The old dependent and friend of the Santa Cruz family,

Plácido Estupiñá, is modelled, we are told by Galdós himself (*16*, II, pp. 201-2), on a stall-holder in the Plaza Mayor called José Luengo. So far, so good. But what really matters is which of the innumerable traits possessed by any human being Galdós has taken over, which he has discarded, how he has organized them and what he has added. Luengo very probably had many of Estupiñá's qualities such as his unquenchable loquacity, his skill at barter, his religious convictions and so on; he may well have lived in the Cava de San Miguel, jeopardized his business by his garrulousness, and provided some of the anecdotes and quirks of speech with which Galdós endowed his character. But none of the foregoing explains the way in which Galdós has integrated him into the action of the novel at various crucial junctures: in visiting him Juanito first becomes acquainted with Fortunata; and he is the instrument by which Fortunata's baby is passed to Jacinta. Even on the level of characterization, it is what is added that is significant. Possible Luengo may have claimed visual acquaintance with the whole succession of key public figures of the nineteenth century but it is Galdós who has given this facet of his character, real or imagined, the structural significance it undoubtedly has in the story. Moreover, he links him with a much more eminent Madrilenian, the *costumbrista* writer Ramón de Mesonero Romanos, to whom Galdós owed so much of his historical information. He gives Estupiñá the same date of birth and makes him look like the composer Rossini, whose resemblance to Mesonero Galdós had noted elsewhere.[8] By bringing together imaginatively in one economical stroke two eminent sons of Madrid, one real and one fictional, the novelist shows how much more there is to writing novels than incorporating random slices of life into his text. It is interesting to note that this feature came to Galdós late in the creative process, for in the manuscript of the novel Estupiñá's birth is made to coincide, much less appropriately, with Victor Hugo's (26.11.1802).

Another fallacy which derives from Naturalist theory, and especially from Zola, is that man is so rigidly determined by material and particularly biological forces that characters in a novel are and must be seen to be completely subjugated to their biological make-up and

---

[8]In 'Galería de españoles célebres', from *Recuerdos de Madrid*; see B. Pérez Galdós, *Recuerdos y memorias*, ed. F. C. Sainz de Robles (Madrid, 1975).

physical environment at a given time. 'One and the same determinism ought to rule the stone of the roads and the brain of man.'[9] Galdós undoubtedly accepted the view that men were conditioned by these factors and in certain cases he lays great stress upon them. *El Pitusín*'s behaviour will serve to illustrate the immediate effects of environment, while Maxi's compensation for his physical inadequacies demonstrates the importance of biological considerations. Galdós is however on his guard against an attitude which would deny his characters all free will or which would call into question the ironic arbitrariness of the human condition. For this reason he constantly resists making such causes the sole or the essential determinants of conduct.[10] At times, indeed, he kicks away the base on which genetic criteria in particular could be founded. For example, at the beginning of the second part, he suggests that the Rubín family may be of Jewish origin, but does so on the very dubious authority of Federico Ruiz (elsewhere he gives the Santa Cruz family a *converso*[11] name, but without comment). Then he hints that as a consequence of the flightiness of Doña Maximiliana Llorente, the mother of the three Rubín brothers, they may have different fathers. This would account for their obvious differences, whereas what they have in common could be attributed to their inheritance from their mother. Juan Pablo is said at one point (II, iii, 3, p. 199) to resemble Doña Lupe, his aunt on his father's side; this would establish his legitimate paternity, but proves nothing regarding the other two. On issues of this kind we simply do not know, as one would not know in similar situations in real life. In this way Galdós effectively cuts out any chance of a straight cause-and-effect relationship determined exclusively by environment or heredity.

Cause-and-effect does however occur elsewhere. In the unfolding of history, Galdós seems to discern a kind of providential design,

[9]*Le Roman expérimental*, quoted by E. Pardo Bazán, *La cuestión palpitante* (1882). Compare also Taine's famous formula of *race, milieu* and *moment*.

[10]On this criterion applied to *Miau*, see my 'La figura Villaamil en *Miau*', *Actas del Primer Congreso Internacional de Estudios Galdosianos*, Las Palmas, 1977), pp. 397-413; and *14* (review), pp. 166-8.

[11]Of converted Jewish blood. See J. Caro Baroja, *Los judíos en la España moderna y contemporánea* (Madrid, 1961).

possibly *krausista*, possibly Hegelian in origin.[12] Walter Pattison has linked it tentatively with *War and Peace* (*7*, pp. 90-3). This historical design will determine an inevitable concatenation of events which applies equally to individuals and to societies and whose structure cannot be precisely analysed. Thus the domestic 'restorations' in the novel (III, ii and v) happen, apparently, through the irresistible force of circumstances, just as the political Restoration does:

> Fue de esas cosas que pasan, sin que se pueda determinar cómo pasaron; hechos fatales en la historia de una familia, como lo son sus similares en la historia de los pueblos; hechos que los sabios presienten, que los expertos vaticinan sin poder decir en qué se fundan, y que llegan a ser efectivos sin que se sepa cómo, pues aunque se los sienta venir, no se ve el disimulado mecanismo que los trae. (III, v, 2, p. 362)

Similarly inevitable, we are told, is Fortunata's acceptance of Feijoo's protection earlier on:

> Como lo que debe suceder, sucede, y no hay bromas con la realidad, las cosas vinieron y ocurrieron conforme a los deseos de don Evaristo González Feijoo . . . Lo que tenía que llegar, por la sucesión infalible de las necesidades humanas, llegó. (III, iv, 3, p. 332)

How far, it may be asked, is this deterministic concept part and parcel of Galdós's total historical attitude? Hans Hinterhäuser has argued that it is based on three principles. According to this view:

1. La Historia es un caminar hacia la perfección, que se realiza como progreso de la 'civilización';
2. Su resultado es la paulatina realización de la libertad;
3. En el desarrollo histórico se cumple un plan de la Providencia. (*2*, p. 117)

These ideas might seem to amount to an unacceptably optimistic doctrine of perfectability of a rather smug nineteenth-century sort, but as Hinterhäuser has pointed out, 'la fe en el progreso y en el plan de la Providencia es el último recurso al que acude el autor antes de llegar a la desesperación' (p. 118). Altogether, he would appear to have a cautiously optimistic view of mankind experiencing 'una

---

[12]*Krausismo* was a highly influential idealistic philosophic movement remotely based on the theories of K. C. F. Krause (1781-1832). See J. López-Morillas, *El krausismo español* (Mexico City, 1956). The German philosopher Hegel (1770-1831) put forward a view of history based on the dialectic of opposites, by which from a thesis and its opposing antithesis a synthesis emerged. See *2*, pp. 115-29, and *13*, pp. 138-50.

evolución lentísima, aunque constante, hasta alcanzar la "plenitud de los tiempos" ' (p. 119). This I would accept as a reasonably accurate assessment of Galdós's view of history in the 1880s, as far as it can be ascertained. Since however the narrative voice must always be borne in mind (see pp. 39-42, below), we should resist the temptation to deduce a clear-cut philosophy of history from the novel. All we should say is that this type of historical causality, crude and mechanistic though it may be, fits admirably the ideological tone adopted by the narrator.

It is clearly impossible within the scope of this brief guide to attempt to cover all aspects of an extremely rich and inexhaustible novel. I shall confine myself therefore to dealing briefly and selectively with certain salient features under the following heads: first, the overall structure of the book; next the modes of presentation by means of the narrator, style, dialogue, etc.; then the depiction of society and environment in nineteenth-century Madrid, followed by an examination of how the characters, minor and major, are portrayed. Lastly, I shall examine in greater depth three major areas of interaction between the principal characters: the clash of Fortunata and Jacinta; the course of Maxi's madness as Fortunata's attitude to him fluctuates; and, finally, the resolution of conflicts as the novel reaches its end.

The first edition of *Fortunata y Jacinta* had 1766 pages in all, distributed approximately equally over the four volumes (volume I is rather longer and volume III rather shorter than the average). The whole novel has 31 chapters, each divided into sections, making a total of 188; eleven chapters (44 sections) in Part I, seven chapters (52 sections) in Part II, seven chapters (42 sections) in Part III and six chapters (50 sections) in Part IV. There is no attempt therefore at structural symmetry of an external kind,[13] and the number of sections within each chapter varies enormously from two in Chapters i and iv in Part I, to twelve in II, vii and IV, i, and sixteen in the final chapter of the book, IV, vi.

Every chapter has its title and is a substantial and carefully organized unit which deals with an important issue. A few of the divisions emerge late in the creative process, and such characteristic titles as 'Escenas de la vida íntima' (II, viii), 'La idea . . . la pícara idea' (III, vii) and 'En la calle del Ave María' (IV, i) are not added till galley proof stage; one chapter, entitled 'La tremenda', and consisting of the present II, vii, 10-12, is dropped at that time and fused with the previous chapter. The sections are even more fluid, and many of them are introduced into the already completed text of the manuscript. Often they do not represent a marked change of scene or subject, but simply a slight pause in the development. At times indeed Galdós maintains the impetus of his story by interrupting it dramatically in full spate with a new section. Thus, when Juanito is explaining to Jacinta how he met Fortunata (I, v, 1-2):

> uno de estos amigos . . . encontró a una mujer que se estaba comiendo un huevo crudo . . . ¿Qué tal? . . .

[2]

—Un huevo crudo . . . ¡Qué asco! —exclamó Jacinta . . . (49) Later when Jacinta questions her husband on the authenticity of *el Pitusín* (I, x, 6-7), the discussion is carried across a section division,

[13]In his *Galdós and Beethoven: 'Fortunata y Jacinta', a symphonic novel* (London, 1977), which appeared after this guide was completed, Vernon A. Chamberlin has suggested that the structure of the novel is modelled on Beethoven's Third (*Eroica*) Symphony. I find the argument entirely unconvincing.

thus reflecting Jacinta's anxiety:
> Pero es tarde, hija mía, nos acostaremos, dormiremos, y maña-
> na. . .

[7]

> —No, no, no— gritó Jacinta, . . . (143)

The encounter between Feijoo and Maxi when the former prepares the ground for the reconciliation with Fortunata (III, iv, 8-9) runs on from one section to another:
> Y abriéndose paso, salió con el chico de Rubín.

[9]

> Al cual dijo en la puerta:
> —¿Hacia dónde va usted con su cuerpo? (349)

The technique, like so much in Galdós, is Cervantine, and it is intended, not only to give flexibility and variety to the narrative pattern, but to draw special attention to the matter which is interrupted.

The title in its full form *Fortunata y Jacinta (dos historias de casadas)* gives a succinct idea of its principal figures: two married women, with their husbands, Juan Santa Cruz and Maximiliano Rubín: thus four main characters. It is perhaps worth noting the form of the sub-title: '*dos* historias . . .', not 'historia de dos casadas': there is an indication here that the stories are to unfold independently, as indeed at the outset they do. Behind the four main characters stand others who as well as furthering the action have highly developed personalities of their own: Doña Guillermina Pacheco, Doña Lupe 'la de los pavos', Mauricia *la dura* and Don Evaristo González Feijoo are especially important. Two other well-developed characters, Moreno-Isla and Segismundo Ballester, have a clear but circumscribed relevance for the two heroines, the former concerned with Jacinta and the latter with Fortunata. Aurora Samaniego is sharply characterized as well as being functionally crucial. There are a multitude of support characters such as Juanito's parents Don Baldomero and Doña Barbarita, Maxi's brothers Juan Pablo and Nicolás, Papitos, Doña Lupe's servant, and the latter's associate Torquemada and Fortunata's uncle José Izquierdo. Some of the support figures like Estupiñá and Ido del Sagrario, and to a lesser extent Villalonga, have the additional significance of being link characters between various sections of society.

Montesinos calls it 'una selva de novelas entrecruzadas', with some reason, though the observation perhaps tends to obscure the clear overall pattern. He goes on to discern three, or possibly four, interwoven novels:

> Las dos primeras quedan perfectamente delimitadas y redondeadas: la de las bodas de Juanito Santa Cruz . . . la segunda es la del casamiento de Fortunata con Maximiliano. La tercera es más difícilmente discernible, pues en las dos últimas partes la materia se entremezcla de modo más complejo, pero como en esos libros descuellan nuevamente Fortunata y Maximiliano digamos que contienen la pasión y muerte de la mujer y la pasión y enloquecimiento del marido, culminante aquélla en el episodio de la maternidad de la heroína. (*16*, II, p. 205)

This again is true enough, so long as the constant interaction is kept in mind.

Galdós is careful to develop separately, in a methodical and leisurely fashion, each of the main branches of his subject: there is a deliberate working out of one theme in depth before he passes to the next. Each part begins by introducing one of the four principal male characters. Thus Book I begins with Juanito Santa Cruz, Book II with Maximiliano Rubín, and Books III and IV, with lesser but still significant figures, Feijoo and Ballester respectively. By contrast, all the female characters, including even the eponymous heroines, are introduced more gradually. It is nonetheless true, though, that Part I gives the first *historia de casada*, Jacinta's. All the circumstances of her family and more particularly of her husband's parents and of their rise to prosperity are retailed in loving detail. They will not receive the same prominence again in the novel, but the author can count henceforth on his reader's close familiarity with the Santa Cruz family circle. Galdós is careful to restrain himself from anticipating events: neither of the other pair, Maximiliano Rubín and Fortunata, takes any part in the first book. Maxi does not intervene at all, and apart from a fleeting glimpse of her in the fine scene when Juanito meets her for the first time, Fortunata is pictured only indirectly, as she emerges in Juanito's confessions to his wife during their honeymoon and in Villalonga's account of her to Juanito. The setting is mainly in the Santa Cruz household, but with an important excursion to the slums by Jacinta and Doña Guillermina in their quest for Juanito's supposed son. The basically unsatisfactory nature of the outwardly happy marriage is clear by the end of the book; and Juanito's renewed search for Fortunata leaves the narrative inconclusive: the last chapter heading is 'Final que viene a ser principio'.

Part II relates the second *historia de casada* with a similarly detailed account of the Rubín family, of Doña Lupe and her three nephews, into which Fortunata enters by marrying Maxi after a period of rehabilitation in the convent-reformatory of Las Micaelas. Apart from this last episode, the action is centred on Doña Lupe's home and the Rubín couple's nearby flat. Juanito now appears only incidentally as the disrupter of the marriage who seduces Fortunata once more and assaults her unfortunate husband; Jacinta takes no real part in this book.

The second book brings some themes to fulfilment; Fortunata's renewed affair with Juanito complements his search for her at the end of Part I and produces an apparently irrevocable break with the Rubín family, but it is evident that no final solution has yet been reached.

So far the novel has developed in a separate but parallel fashion. As Montesinos pointed out, Parts III and IV are less clear-cut. To the Santa Cruz and Rubín residences are added other settings: the cafés frequented by Juan Pablo Rubín and his friends, the apartment of Fortunata's benevolent protector Feijoo and the tenement dwellings of the 'Cuarto Estado'. Fortunata and Maxi have come to command our attention, however, and only one chapter in each book directly involves the Santa Cruz household: the confrontation and temporary reconciliation of Juanito and Jacinta in III, ii, and the episode of Moreno-Isla's death in IV, ii.

Apart from the café scenes, Part III brings various influences to bear on Fortunata, who now dominates the course of the novel. When she is deserted by Juanito, Feijoo counsels moderation and arranges her reunion with Maxi. Mauricia stresses her right to love and Doña Guillermina urges sacrifice. She confronts Jacinta for the first time. In resuming her liaison with Juanito she becomes possessed by a project ('la pícara idea') of her own, that of bearing his child.

In Part IV Fortunata's personality reaches its full development as she achieves her object of having a child by Juanito. She can count on the devotion of a new admirer, Segismundo. Following Fortunata's attack on Aurora, Juanito's new lover, and her subsequent death, a posthumous spiritual reconciliation with Jacinta ensues. But Maxi's madness —the consequence of his matrimonial disaster— claims just as much attention and the final words of the novel are his.

Despite the demarcations, the novel is a united whole. The implications of the *Pitusín* episode of Part I are picked up in the last, when a true son of Juanito's is adopted by Jacinta from the 'Cuarto Estado'. Fortunata's idea of swapping a *nene chico* for a *nene grande* is fulfilled in an unexpected way. The names given to the baby —Juan Evaristo Segismundo— perpetuate in no uncertain fashion the influences on his mother's life of each of these three men. As for Maxi, his yearning to break out of his intolerable situation by death or abstraction is fulfilled on the death of his wife.

In a perceptive study (*31*, pp. 137-59) Ricardo Gullón has described the structural technique of *Fortunata y Jacinta*. He sees the development of the love theme as one of changing triangles: Juanito, Jacinta, Fortunata; followed by Juanito, Fortunata, Maxi; Fortunata, Maxi, Feijoo; Juan, Fortunata, Aurora; and finally, Fortunata, Jacinta, Juanito (p. 138), with Fortunata now occupying the key position. She is the one constant in all the triangles, so that what this geometrical pattern in fact signifies is that the axis of the novel as it unfolds is Fortunata. All the major secondary characters have a direct relation with Fortunata, even if they belong initially to other spheres: thus Doña Guillermina, who is clearly a member of Jacinta's world, comes to have a major impact on Fortunata, whereas Doña Lupe intervenes no less in the life of Fortunata than in that of her nephew; the relations of Mauricia, Feijoo and Ballester with Fortunata are even more direct. As Sherman Eoff points out, 'this conception of personality as an interaction between the individual and the social units with which he is inseparably linked is one of the outstanding features of Galdós' character portrayal' (*13*, p. 55). Altogether, Galdós has achieved a difficult balance between diversity and unity; rather than three or four novels, as Montesinos has it, Galdós has related successively various facets of two distinct family histories, gradually concentrating increasing attention on the woman who provides a link between them and uniting the two stories at the end, after the death of Fortunata.

Among the other structural threads running through the novel are the polarity between Doña Guillermina and Mauricia, also noted by Gullón (*31*, pp. 159-67) and the technique of 'ironic reprise' carefully described by Monroe Z. Hafter (*15*, pp. 235-7). This interior duplication can be found between the two bachelor admirers of the heroines, Feijoo and Moreno-Isla, in the similarity of the deaths of Mauricia and Fortunata, and in the parallel between Maxi and José Ido (*22*, pp. 222-3). These issues will be discussed in greater detail later.

Consistency of imagery also makes for unity. Several critics, starting with Stephen Gilman (*40, 41*) and continuing with Roger L. Utt (*32*) and Agnes Moncy Gullón (*30*) have pointed to the remarkable quantity of bird imagery in the novel. Even after a large number of instances have been discounted as incidental or normal colloquial usage, there still remain many which add up to a consistent metaphorical pattern. Whether this goes beyond the sort of technique of animal comparison so prevalent in *Miau* is an open question. The association of Fortunata with the 'pájara mala' in *Doña Desdémona*'s aviary is structurally significant with regard to Maxi who is still ruminating about killing Fortunata:

    ¡Qué mala es esta pájara! –decía *Doña Desdémona*–. No sabe usted lo mala que es. Ha matado ya tres maridos . . .
    La lógica exige su muerte –pensaba Rubín, colgando cuidadosamente una jaula en que había muchos nidos– (IV, v, 3, p. 492)

and is explicit in the message sent via Maxi to Doña Lupe: 'la pájara mala sacó pollo esta mañana'(IV, v, 4, p. 497)

Jacinta, for her part, is described on various occasions as a *paloma* driven into a state of rage (I, viii, 5, p. 95; I, x, 2, p. 130; III, vii, 3, p. 407), and this offers effective support to the portrayal of her character. A case can also be made that Fortunata is consistently compared to a hen from her first meeting with Juanito, but this comparison does not seem to me to add greatly to the novel. Whether or not the many references to eating or hatching eggs (I, iii, 4, p. 41; IV, vi, 2, p. 505), to the fried birds the honeymoon couple consume (I, v, 4, p. 55) or to Fortunata's claim to be an angel can be related to this imagery is more doubtful; they introduce an element which is both mechanical and incongruous into a work more noteworthy for lively characterization than for a rigid symbolic pattern: A. M. Gullón (*30*) exaggerates in my view the structural intricacy of the novel. The most I consider justifiable is to accept Utt's modest claim that there is 'potencial simbólico latente en su expresión espontánea'. He goes on:

> Estas expresiones, precisamente por ser propiedad del habla corriente, por no 'oler a literatura', no llaman la atención del lector; sin embargo, no pueden dejar de manifestar una capacidad simbólica que añade otra dimensión al personaje de Jacinta (= la dulce paloma enrabiada) con respecto a Fortunata (= la mala pájara, tosca, enjaulada, sofocada). (*32*, p. 47)

Other motifs also contribute to the unity of structure. The *noria* or wind-pump which operates outside Las Micaelas has a reassuring or depressing effect on Maxi (see p. 54), though it does not appear to me closely connected with the bird imagery as Utt claims (*32*, pp. 37-40). The superstition of the buttons which Mauricia instils into Fortunata has its structural importance in her relations with Juanito (*31*, p. 172; see p. 97). As we shall see in the course of this study, dreams (see Schraibman, *21* and *18*) and visions frequently have a prophetic or reiterative function.

Galdós has taken care to fix his novel firmly in both time and space. In the first pages Juanito Santa Cruz and his companions emerge as university students in the 1860s (in other words, they are approximately the same age as Galdós at that period): they take part in the savagely suppressed demonstrations of the *noche de San Daniel* (10 April 1865), in which Galdós himself was involved. The narrative proper starts in 1869, when Santa Cruz is 24; in December of that year he pays the visit to the sick Estupiñá which has such far-reaching consequences, setting off a train of events which culminates in Fortunata's death in April 1876. Juanito abandons Fortunata in May 1870, becomes engaged to Jacinta in July and marries her in May 1871. Fortunata meets Maxi in February 1874 and begins her second liaison with Juanito immediately after her marriage in September of that year. The affair lasts only until the Restoration, in January 1875, when Feijoo takes her under his wing for about two months. The reconciliation with Maxi occurs in Spring 1875 and the affair with Juanito is resumed a few weeks later, lasting till Autumn that year. In December she leaves Maxi to return to the Cava de San Miguel where she has her baby in April

1876 and dies shortly afterwards. Some critics, notably Montesinos (*16*, II, p. 266) have complained that the action is too precipitate, but in my view both Juanito's fickleness and Feijoo's sudden decline are perfectly plausible. The key political events of this turbulent period following the Revolution of September 1868 are recalled and even integrated into the story (*12*, pp. 134-44). The characters of *Fortunata*, no less than those of *Le Rouge et le Noir*, can be said to be 'embedded in a total reality, political, social, economic, which is concrete and constantly evolving'.[14] The assassination of the most determined opponent of the Bourbon dynasty, General Juan Prim, in December 1870; the abdication of King Amadeo in February 1873; the outbreak of the Carlist War (II, i, 1, p. 160) and subsequent engagements as reflected in Juan Pablo Rubín's *tertulia* (III, i, 3); the military coup of General Pavía, which dealt a death blow to the First Republic, in January 1874; and the return of the Bourbon Alfonso XII in January 1875 all figure prominently (*1*, pp. 305-46). In a fine scene (I, xi, 1-2), Villalonga alternates between a description of Fortunata for Juanito's benefit and an account, once Jacinta enters the room, of the dramatic invasion of the *Cortes* by Pavía's troops: as has been pointed out elsewhere (*37*, pp. 94-105) the swing of the pendulum between revolution and consolidation in Spanish politics is paralleled by the alternation in Juanito Santa Cruz's affections. The political terms 'revolución' and 'restauración' are used in three chapter headings (ii, iii, and v) in Part III for the private affairs of the two couples. The Restoration brings about a reconciliation of interests through weariness rather than conviction, which produces an easing of political tension and opportunities for advancement through influence and patronage. This atmosphere is excellently captured in a description of café politics:

> Allí brillaba espléndidamente esa fraternidad española en cuyo seno se dan mano de amigo el carlista y el republicano, el progresista de cabeza dura y el moderado implacable. Antiguamente, los partidos separados en público, estábanlo también en las relaciones privadas; pero el progreso de las costumbres trajo primero cierta suavidad en las relaciones personales, y, por fin, la suavidad se trocó en blandura. Algunos creen que hemos pasado de un

---

[14]Erich Auerbach, *Mimesis* (Princeton, 1953), p. 463.

extremado mal a otro, sin detenernos en el medio conveniente, y ven en esta fraternidad una relajación de los caracteres. Esto de que todo el mundo sea amigo particular de todo el mundo es síntoma de que las ideas van siendo tan sólo un pretexto para conquistar o defender el pan. Existe una confabulación tácita (no tan escondida que no se encuentre a poco que se rasque en los políticos), por la cual se establece el turno en el dominio. En esto consiste que no hay aspiración, por extraviada que sea, que no se tenga por probable; en esto consiste la inseguridad, única cosa que es constante entre nosotros; la ayuda masónica que se prestan todos los partidos, desde el clerical al anarquista, lo mismo dándose una credencial vergonzante en tiempo de paces que otorgándose perdones e indultos en las guerras y revoluciones. Hay algo de seguros mutuos contra el castigo, razón por la cual se miran los hechos de fuerza como la cosa más natural del mundo. La moral política es como una capa con tantos remiendos, que no se sabe ya cuál es el paño primitivo. (III, i, 1, pp. 294-5)

No less important to Galdós than the contemporary political situation is the economic background, which I shall discuss in the chapter on 'Depiction of Society'.

Galdós, as befits the chronicler of early nineteenth-century history in the *episodios nacionales*, is also concerned to recall the essential historical facts of the immediate past. This he accomplishes by means of two minor characters, Estupiñá and Doña Isabel Cordero, Jacinta's mother. Old Estupiñá claimed to have witnessed the whole of Spanish history from the beginning of the century; among others, he had seen such temporary rulers of Spain's destiny as Joseph I, Napoleon's brother; the Duke of Wellington, during the Peninsular War; Ferdinand VII cowed by the militia (7 July 1822); the Duke of Angoulême, leader of the French absolutist invasion of 1823; the new queen María Cristina entering Madrid in 1829; the fall of her regency on 1 September 1840; the political generals of Isabella II's reign, O'Donnell and Espartero; and finally the expulsion of the Bourbons by Prim in 1868. His experience was limited to the superficial political manifestations of the country: 'la historia que Estupiñá sabía estaba escrito en los balcones' (I, iii, 1, p. 35), but he provides evidence of its unsettled state since the Napoleonic invasion. For her part Doña Isabel Cordero de Arnáiz, daughter of the hero of several *episodios nacionales*, Benigno Cordero, marked by means of her prodigious fecundity the 'fechas célebres' of the reign of her namesake Isabella II (reigned 1833-1868):

— Mi primer hijo — decía — nació cuando vino la tropa carlista
hasta las tapias de Madrid [September 1837]. Mi Jacinta nació
cuando se casó la reina [10 October 1846] con pocos días de
diferencia. Mi Isabelita vino al mundo el día mismo en que el
cura Merino le pegó la puñalada a su majestad [2 February 1852],
y tuve a Rupertito el día de San Juan [i.e. 24 June] del 58, el
mismo día que se inauguró la traída de aguas. (I, ii, 6, p. 31.
See *1*, pp. 79-304)

Even in her death she is pursued by 'fechas célebres', for she died
on the same day (30 December 1870) as Prim was assassinated by
unknown hands. The engagement of Juanito and Jacinta, which has
just been arranged, is thus linked to the crucial event which ruined
the chances of success of the incoming constitutional monarch
Amadeo of Savoy (*37*, pp. 91-3).

Fortunata y Jacinta is equally specific and detailed regarding
space. Apart from the honeymoon of the young Santa Cruz couple,
the whole action takes place in Madrid (see maps on pp.34-6). The
Santa Cruz family, senior and junior, live together in an imposing
patrician house, still standing in the Calle de Pontejos, near the Puerta
del Sol; next door lived Doña Guillermina and her nephew Moreno-
Isla. Fortunata was born and died in an apartment in the Cava de
San Miguel, no. 11, a massive stone tenement building which forms
one side of the Plaza Mayor; Estupiñá had the top flat in the same
building, at the top of a staircase of 120 steps. Galdós clearly had
personal knowledge of both these dwellings, for his information,
minor details apart, is remarkably accurate and precise. Severiana
and the Ido family live in one of the squalid slum blocks (Mira el
Río Alta 12) to the South of the Plaza Mayor; this is where Mauricia
died. Doña Lupe and her family first reside in the new Barrio de
Salamanca (*Pajaritos*, now the Calle de Ayala), later in the equally
new but less stylish district of Chamberí (Calle de Raimundo Lulio),
both in the North of the city, and finally in the Calle del Ave María,
near Samaniego's pharmacy, in the South. The convent of Las
Micaelas, though not modelled on a real establishment,[15] is also
situated, like most of the new religious foundations, in the North;

[15]For this and other information about the Madrid of *Fortunata*, I am indebted
to the Christmas greeting booklets devoted to this subject by D. Pedro Ortiz
Armengol (see also *25*).

Doña Guillermina's half-finished orphanage is in the Calle de Alburquerque, very near Doña Lupe's second apartment.

Altogether, the novel is full of topographical detail resulting from an extraordinary and affectionate intimacy with the streets and popular life of Madrid. Some awareness of its urban geography enhances our appreciation of Galdós's fictional world. First, a couple of examples where distance is involved. We can picture José Ido, instructed to carry some 70 bricks by hand from the gasometer on the southern outskirts of Madrid to Doña Guillermina's orphanage in Chamberí. It is a distance of some eight kilometres and the unfortunate Ido no doubt had to make several journeys with his load. Second, two contrasting walks by Fortunata; the first (II, vii, 5, pp. 275-6) along the broad avenue, Santa Engracia (now the Calle de Joaquín García Morato), near her home —'¡Qué gusto poder coger de punta a punta una calle tan larga . . .!'— as she meditates on her profound dissatisfaction with her recent marriage and the perversity of fate that the man she loved was not a simple workman; the second (III, iii, 2), when, abandoned for the second time by Juanito, she went, distraught and powerless, to peer at the Santa Cruz mansion, sat for a time by the fountain in the Puerta del Sol and was then encountered nearby by Feijoo; the wandering route she took underlines her disorientation.

Social contrasts are also underlined by local geography. The journey Jacinta makes with Guillermina through the bustling street-market of Calle de Toledo to see José Izquierdo about *el Pitusín* (I, ix, 1) reveals a degree of activity, colour and squalor which serves to indicate the very different worlds which co-exist within a very small area of the city. Other examples have more subjective con-notations. The demolition of the church-tower of Santa Cruz in 1869, so closely associated with the Arnáiz and Santa Cruz families (Don Baldomero and Barbarita were married there), was a special blow to pious old Estupiñá, who always took off his hat and crossed himself whenever he passed the site. The district where Feijoo lived (Calle de Don Pedro, Puerta de Moros), though not very far from the centre, was just outside the old shell of the city. It was therefore regarded as outlandishly distant by traditional Madrilenians. Its seclusion suited admirably Feijoo's purpose of keeping up appear-ances when he installed Fortunata in a modest room in a nearby

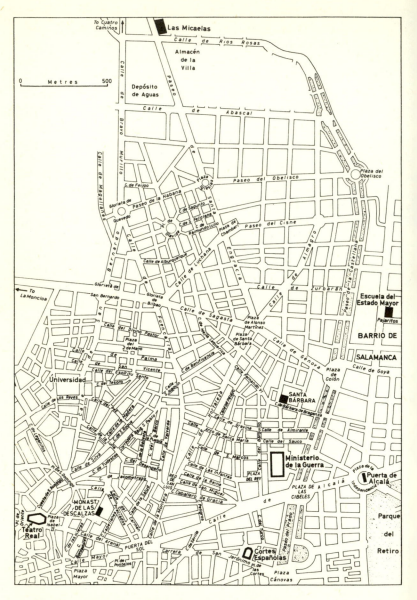

a: Northern suburbs of Madrid in the late 19th Century.

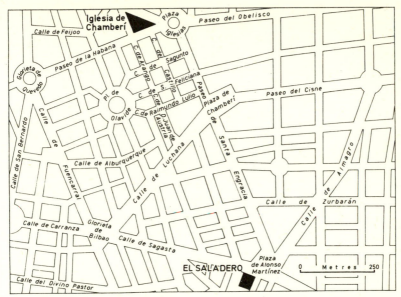

b: *The district of Chamberí*

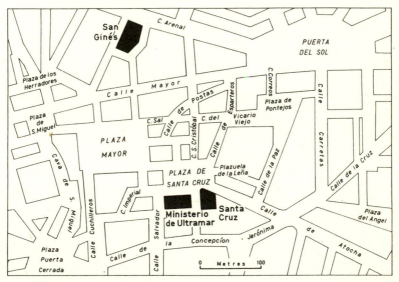

c: *The area of the Plaza Mayor*

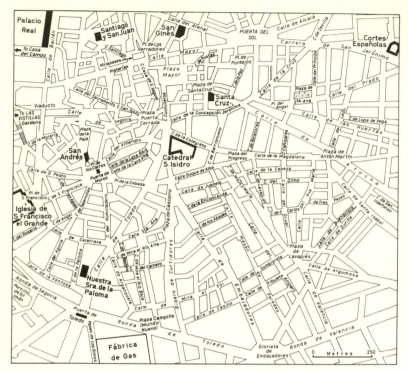

d: Southern suburbs of Madrid in the late 19th Century.

street (Calle de Tabernillas). The shortish distance between this house and the Plaza Mayor serves also as the measure of Feijoo's physical decline (III, iv, 6, 340) when he is obliged to take a carriage from the Plaza to get there. All in all, Galdós succeeds admirably in blending local urban geography with the private lives of his characters in a positive functional way. His profound feeling for place is an essential part of his realistic presentation of individuals and society.

III Modes of presentation

The importance of the narrative approach adopted by the novelist cannot be over-emphasized. The omniscient unobtrusive narrator favoured by the realists and naturalists easily loses credibility because he knows more than he possibly could about the inner thoughts or secret actions of the characters. On the other hand, once a personal narrator is introduced, whether he is the protagonist, an important character or simply an observer on the sidelines, he becomes prone to human fallibility and his reliability can be called into question. Galdós is very well aware of these problems and in a succession of novels chooses varying solutions for them: *El amigo Manso* and *Lo prohibido* are, in quite different ways, first-person narratives. *La desheredada*, *El doctor Centeno* and *Tormento* have no personal narrators but increasingly, in the latter novels, the role of José Ido casts doubt on the reliability of the narrator. *La de Bringas*, by contrast, has a dramatized but unnamed narrator who plays a not inconsiderable part in the action, especially in the final stages of the novel. *Fortunata y Jacinta* follows a similar pattern, although it is easier in this case to ignore or mistake the role of the narrator, so inconspicuous is he. Unnamed, of a similar age and social status to Juanito Santa Cruz and his companions, an unwary reader may easily take him for Galdós himself (see *28*, pp. 118-19). This is a fundamental error, since it will equate the author with the attitude of his characters, or of some of them, whereas it is the independently portrayed, though shadowy, figure of the narrator who is made to share this attitude. Rather than adopt the technique of having a third-person omniscient narrator, either of the neutral kind who does not comment off his own bat on the activities of the characters or of the obtrusive variety favoured by Fielding, Trollope and Tolstoy, Galdós has chosen a narrator who claims acquaintance with a number of characters and who is in many instances careful to explain the sources of his knowledge; he is a witness, direct or indirect, of many of the main events. Real occurrences drawn from Galdós's own experience —attendance at the lectures of the highly esteemed professor of Latin, Camús, participation in the *noche de San Daniel*— are mingled with fictitious events. At the same time the narrator indulges in the same type of pseudo-confidential asides to the reader which are found in Fielding or Trollope. One of the clearest examples is the episode of Mauricia's drunken riot following the hunt for a mouse in Sor Marcela's cell. It begins:

> Es cosa muy cargante para el historiador verse obligado a hacer mención de muchos pormenores y circunstancias enteramente pueriles y que más bien han de excitar el desdén que la curiosidad del que lee, pues aunque luego resulte que estas nimiedades tienen su engranaje efectivo en la máquina de los acontecimientos, no por esto parecen dignas de que se las traiga a cuento en una relación verídica y grave. Ved, pues, por qué pienso que se han de reír los que lean aquí ahora que sor Marcela tenía miedo a los ratones. (II, vi, 8, p. 249)

Such interventions occur, however, from within the fictional environment portrayed, and at least some of the advantages sought by Henry James in his use of one of his characters as a 'reflector'[16] are secured.

By putting his narrator, however marginally, into the same environment as that of a group of his characters, the novelist endows him to some extent with the same preoccupations and prejudices, the same limited knowledge and the same liability to error as his fellows, while exempting the author *qua* author from identification with these views. He becomes therefore in some degree the 'unreliable narrator' described by Wayne Booth (*Rhetoric of Fiction*, pp. 158-65).

From the very first sentence of the novel the personal, but necessarily limited and second-hand, sources of the narrator's information are stressed:

> Las noticias más remotas que tengo de la persona que lleva este nombre [Juanito Santa Cruz] me las ha dado Jacinto María Villalonga, y alcanzan al tiempo en que este amigo mío y el otro y el de más allá, Zalamero, Joaquinito Pez, Alejandro Miquis, iban a las asulas de la Universidad. (I, i, 1, p. 13)

Our narrator subsequently claims acquaintanceship with many of the principal characters, noting in most cases the date he met them: Juanito about 1869, Don Baldomero and Doña Barbarita in 1870. He has often seen Doña Bárbara and Jacinta shopping together

---

[16]For the whole subject of narrative technique see Norman Friedman, 'Point of View in Fiction: the development of a critical concept', *Publications of the Modern Language Association*, LXX (1955), 1160-84, and Wayne C. Booth, *The Rhetoric of Fiction* (Chicago, 1961).

(I, vi, 1, p. 64). In the case of Estupiñá, he says on one occasion that he met him when he was nearing 70, on another, in 1871; the slight uncertainty —Estupiñá's seventieth birthday is given as 19 July 1873— lending greater plausibility to a story depending on the narrator's memory. This acquaintance with the garrulous Plácido justifies the narrator's intimate knowledge of the world of commerce and of the Santa Cruz and Arnáiz families; he credits his detailed description of the development of the Madrid drapery trade to a conversation between Estupiñá and Arnáiz (I, vi, 1, p. 66). Zalamero, likewise, is responsible for providing details regarding Doña Guillermina's early life (I, vi, 1, p. 76), whilst information on the visit to the 'Cuarto Estado' is provided by Rafaela (I, ix, 7, p. 117).

It is inevitable, therefore, that the personal narrator's knowledge should be relative and incomplete (*31*, pp. 205-9). There is no reason to doubt the facts he gives us, but at times we have no means of assessing exactly what happened. Who were Juanito's mistresses before he resumed his liaison with Fortunata? Is Maxi completely impotent? What circumstances first caused Mauricia's attacks or her alcoholism? Did Feijoo ever pay court to Doña Lupe? Were Aurora's relations with Moreno-Isla as she described them? Galdós's narrative technique leaves ample scope for the ambiguities he so delighted in.

Equally important is the narrative tone this technique enables Galdós to adopt. From the beginning the narrator writes, not as an outside observer, but as a friendly commentator on the sidelines. He displays throughout a genial, compromising, give-and-take attitude. He is very close ideologically to the prosperous bourgeoisie he is describing and the world they live in without being deeply committed; he is sympathetic yet detached. James Whiston has defined this narrative position very well:

It establishes his detachment and magnanimity at the level of the social action, while in the half-conscious regions of metaphor especially and also in sentence structure we can see the tension between magnanimous acceptance and the doubts and ironies which he hems around the making of narrative value judgments. (*35*, p. 79)

As a result of the point of view of the narrator, the novel is focused initially on this prosperous commercial world, which is portrayed as natural and its values as self-evident. As a consequence his opinions have no absolute authority, for his judgements come from within the society he is describing. Certainly, he does not conceal his views, but they are the expected ones of his class, not objective value judgements from outside and above. He rebukes Barbarita in apparently strong terms for her insensitivity in poking fun at her daughter-in-law's yearning for a child, but then dampens its effect by passing rapidly on to speak of the former's own *chifladura*: her craze for shopping, by contrast so easily satisfied.

> Hacía muy mal Barbarita, pero muy mal, en burlarse de la manía de su hija. ¡Como si ella no tuviera también su manía, y buena! (I, vi, 5, p. 72)

A more far-reaching example is provided by Juanito's upbringing. The quite obvious mollycoddling of their son by the Santa Cruz couple is constantly played down by the narrator. On more than one occasion we are told, against all the evidence, that he was not spoilt, that he was brought up *sin mimo*: '[Barbarita] no trataba a su hijo con mimo. Su ternura sabía ser inteligente y revestirse a veces de severidad dulce' (I, i, 1, p. 15). Even apart from the tell-tale *a veces*, what in fact this implies, once the narrator's favourable gloss is removed and due allowance made for Galdós's irony, is that Barbarita's absorbing motherly despotism did much to ensure that Juanito developed no sense of responsibility as well as acquiring a taste for gratifying every whim. Likewise as Don Baldomero's excessive indulgences are apparently curbed by his wife we realize to what extent their long-awaited only son was in fact pampered. In the case of Juanito himself, the usual method employed, as we shall see later, is to express a moderate criticism and then hasten to qualify it. As actions are allowed to speak for themselves, the reader becomes accustomed to reading between the lines and discounting the surface opinions expressed by the narrator. This is the tone which prevails in Part I, and it is this tone, it seems to me, which enables Galdós to make certain general statements about historical laws (see p. 20) and about society and *el pueblo* which we shall discuss later (pp. 69-70). The latter are the accepted truths of the society of which both the narrator and the Santa Cruz's form part, but are not to be taken as any absolute norm as they might have been had they come from an omniscient narrator.

It is worth noticing, moreover, that the time scale adopted contributes to this same atmosphere of detached familiarity. The narrator is deemed to be writing some fifteen years after the earliest events recounted at the end of 1869, that is to say, very nearly co-inciding with the actual time of composition of the novel. The span of time involved produces a due sense of distance and a certain nostalgic glow about events occurring in the immediate past which have consequences continuing into the present. To emphasize this, the narrator makes sure to tell us that Don Baldomero and Barbarita are happily still alive. And he comments complacently on Juanito's escapades in the light of the present, in the established manner of those who from time immemorial deplore the decline of their own times: 'En esto, como en todo lo malo, hemos progresado de tal modo, que las barrabasadas de aquel niño bonito hace quince años nos parecerían hoy timideces y aun actos de ejemplaridad relativa' (I, i, 2, p. 16).

In later books the narrative technique shifts somewhat. Only when the story focuses momentarily once more on the Santa Cruz household (III, ii) does a personal intervention of the narrator still occur, when Jacinta confides in him, and the comments concerning Juanito are notably more critical and more direct. The distance between the narrator and the Santa Cruz world has not unnaturally grown greater as a result of the intervening story of the Rubín family. Although the narrator's personal part in the action after the first part is less evident, his presence continues to be felt. He goes on in the same genial vein, showing considerable acquaintance with the characters and the environment of the Rubín family. About Nicolás's confrontation with Fortunata when her adultery is dis-covered (II, vii, 10, p. 291), we are informed: 'Cuenta el padre Rubín . . .', presumably to the narrator; we could imagine him present at the *tertulias* in Part III; and his friendship with Villalonga could account for his knowledge about Feijoo, Juan Pablo Rubín and the cafés they frequent. These contacts are evidently not sufficient to explain all the detailed knowledge the narrator displays, and from the second part onwards a considerable amount of what Wayne Booth calls authorial 'privilege' (*Rhetoric of Fiction*, pp. 160-3; *28*) is required, but Galdós has already established sufficient associations with the characters to lend both plausibility and the assurance that the narrator knows intimately the people and situations he is talking about. If the narrator's own persona fades into the background, he increasingly allows the characters to speak and act for themselves, or to influence the tone of his narration, with little direct commentary from him.

Linked with the question of narrative tone is the whole subject of stylistic expression. Galdós is of course famous for his concern to employ the actual speech of his characters whenever possible. He was equally conscious of how difficult this task was, given the lack of previous spadework, as he declared in the prologue to Pereda's *El sabor de la tierruca* (1882):

> Una de las mayores dificultades con que tropieza la novela en España consiste en lo poco hecho y trabajado que está el lenguaje literario para reproducir los matices de la conversación corriente. Oradores y poetas lo sostienen en sus antiguos moldes académicos, defendiéndolo de los esfuerzos que hace la conversación para apoderarse de él; el terco régimen aduanero de los cultos le priva de flexibilidad. Por otra parte, la Prensa, con raras excepciones, no se esmera en dar al lenguaje corriente la acentuación literaria y de estas rancias antipatías entre la retórica y la conversación, entre la academia y el periódico, resultan infranqueables diferencias entre *la manera de escribir* y *la manera de hablar*, diferencias que son desesperación y escollo del novelista.[17]

'Clarín' shows a full awareness of Galdós's early achievement in this respect when he praises in *Del estilo en la novela* (1882-3) the naturalness of the dialogue of *El amigo Manso* (see Beser, p. 86).

A considerable part of his text is normally expressed in direct discourse, and some of his works, notably *Realidad*, are written entirely in dialogue, though they are still novels, not plays. This solution, though it underlines the importance Galdós attached to the spoken word, is not in my view a happy one since it seriously impedes the presentation of rounded characters. More subtle techniques are used to better effect in other novels, including *Fortunata y Jacinta*. This is not to say, of course, that there is any lack of sustained dialogue in the novel; good examples are to be found for instance in the honeymoon episode (I, v, 2), between Juanito and Fortunata at the moment of the renewal of their relations at the end of Part III, and in the conversation between Jacinta

[17]See Beser, *Leopoldo Alas*, p. 49.

and Moreno-Isla (IV, ii, 2). In all these cases, however, the narrative structure has prepared the way for the passages of direct speech; there are no cases of whole 'scenes' in dialogue as in *El doctor Centeno* or *Tormento*.

Galdós shows himself a past-master at reflecting varied types of speech patterns (*14*, pp. 240-4; *18*). The skill with which he conveys the infantile amorous speech of the young couple on their honeymoon has been frequently remarked upon. No less successful are other forms of utterance: the distinctive illiterate rhetoric of José Izquierdo's revolutionary fulminations; the racy popular speech laced with swearwords of Mauricia *la dura*; Fortunata's language, direct and equally unpolished, but inhibited by doubts and hesitations; Aurora's gallicisms and Moreno-Isla's anglicisms; the pretentious pomposity of the café pundits.

Meditations and dreams are often reproduced in direct speech and are sometimes extended so far as to become miniature dramatic monologues. At times, as in Fortunata's lengthy reflexions on her rashness in voicing her suspicions of Jacinta to Juanito (IV, iii, 1), Galdós punctuates it with short interpolations ('Comentario', 'Reproducción de algo que ella le había contestado', 'Y él') in the style of stage directions. These monologues are not the exclusive province of the major characters. Doña Lupe has one (IV, v, 5) on the scandal which she thinks will inevitably ensue from Fortunata's pregnancy. Fortunata's fatal attack is graphically presented by means of a dramatic monologue by Estupiñá (IV, vi, 14). Moreno-Isla has an extended meditation during a sleepless night (IV, ii, 3) which is outstanding for the assorted strands of memory which go to make it up. He deliberates first on the tragic irony of his impossible love for Jacinta which he cannot bring himself to express, the desire for a child he shares with her, his misunderstood unhappiness and his heart condition. Then various chance associations pass through his mind, expressed partly in subjectivized narrative and partly in direct speech once more. He thinks compassionately of the deformed beggar he saw that morning; he discovers shapes in the dimly lit objects in the room, while the faint sounds outside bring back recollections of London, of a girl he met there, then of Aurora Fenelón. As he resolves to leave Madrid, his mind reverts constantly to Jacinta, her loyalty to her husband and her opinion of him.

Finally he recalls memories of childhood such as the escapade with a donkey which left a scar on his forehead. Altogether, it is a most remarkable anticipation of the 'stream of consciousness' technique of random associations exemplified by Virginia Woolf and James Joyce.

Other instances of unexplained chance associations also occur. One such example is provided by the casual experiences which bring Fortunata back to Jacinta's mind during her honeymoon (obviously, only the slightest of stimuli are needed to do this):

> Es que hace un rato me dio por pensar en ella. Se me ocurrió de repente. ¿Sabes cómo? Vi unos refajos encarnados puestos a secar en un arbusto. Tú dirás que qué tiene que ver . . . Es claro, nada; pero vete a saber cómo se enlazan en el pensamiento las ideas. Esta mañana me acordé de lo mismo cuando pasaban rechinando las carretillas cargadas de equipajes. Anoche me acordé, ¿cuándo creerás?, cuando apagaste la luz. Me pareció que la llama era una mujer que decía: ' ¡Ay!', y se caía muerta. Ya sé que son tonterías; pero en el cerebro pasan cosas muy particulares. (I, v, 4, p. 56)

Other important monologues belong to Fortunata, the most effective example being the frantic, staccato ejaculations which follow her encounter with Doña Guillermina and Jacinta (III, vii, 4):

> — ¡A mí decirme . . .! Si no me echan, la cojo . . . le levanto . . .; pero no sé, no recuerdo bien si le arañé la cara. ¡A mí decirme . . .! Si le pego un bocado, no la suelto . . . ¡Ja, ja, ja! (p. 408)

She then proceeds in rapid succession to a further denunciation of the childless Jacinta, to a scurrilous attack on Guillermina and a typical confusion of the latter with the dead Mauricia, with whom she longs to drown her sorrows: all in vivid colloquial speech.

The use of direct speech makes for liveliness but does little to further the development of the story. The establishment of a satisfactory narrative style is the first step and 'Clarín' praises Galdós for following Balzac's success in *humillar el estilo* so as to produce a workable implement, 'sencillo, severo, exacto' (see Beser, p. 63), for narration. A more complex problem which has preoccupied many novelists is how to wed the narrative flow to the immediacy of direct discourse. Flaubert is usually credited with the invention of an intermediate stage between the traditionally strictly separated *oratio directa* and *oratio obliqua*. In this intermediate form, free indirect discourse,[18] the introductory clauses like 'he declared' or 'she insisted that' are omitted; the tenses and persons are shifted in order to conform to the narrative but —a very important point— questions and exclamations are retained. The narrator can therefore slip easily into reflecting his characters' point of view without either remaining aloof or intervening directly. On the whole Galdós prefers where possible, as we have seen, to pass straight to direct speech. For this reason he does not use this device as often or as systematically as Flaubert or Alas, but it occurs with very considerable frequency nonetheless, often as a faster-moving variant in combination with direct speech. Pure indirect speech is little used.

A few examples chosen at random clearly reveal the vigour of the spoken language reflected indirectly: Doña Bárbara meditating on the evils of Paris:

> Como que estaba infestada la gran ciudad de unas mujeronas muy guapas y elegantes, que al pronto parecían duquesas, vestidas con los más bonitos y los más nuevos arreos de la moda. Mas cuando se las veía de cerca, resultaban ser unas tiotas relajadas, camilonas, borrachas y ávidas de dinero, que desplumaban y resecaban al pobrecito que en sus garras caía. (I, i, 2, p. 18)

Jacinta, musing on *el Pitusín*:

> Quería llorar; pero ¿qué diría la familia al verla hecha un mar de lágrimas? Habría que decir el motivo . . . Si todo era un embuste, si aquel hombre estaba loco . . . Era autor de novelas de brocha gorda, y no pudiendo ya escribirlas para el público, intentaba llevar a la vida real los productos de su imaginación llena de tuberculosis. Sí, sí, sí: no podía ser otra cosa: tisis de la fantasía. (I, viii, 5, p. 95)

Fortunata, relating her past life to Maxi:

> ¡Cuánto le pesó ponerse en manos de aquel hombre! Era un perdido, un charrán, una mala persona. Hubiérase resistido a seguirle, si no la empujaron a ello los parientes, que no tenían maldita gana de mantenerle el pico . . . No ganaba un cuarto; con el mundo entero armaba camorra, y todo el veneno que iba amasando en su maldecida alma, por la mala suerte, lo descargaba sobre su querida . . . En fin, vida más arrastrada no la había pasado

---

[18]See Stephen Ullmann, *Style in the French Novel* (Cambridge, 1957): 'Reported Speech and Internal Monologue in Flaubert', pp. 117-20. Note particularly 'Free indirect style is reported speech masquerading as narrative. It. . . provides a discreet but effective vehicle for irony and ambiguity, and for the description of reveries, dreams and hallucinatory states' (p. 117).

ella nunca, ni esperaba volverla a pasar . . . (II, ii, 2, p. 175).

Or Fortunata again, contemplating returning to Maxi:

¡Volver con su marido! ¡Ser otra vez la señora de Rubín! . . .
¿Llegaría aquello a ser posible y hasta conveniente? . . . Que
Don Evaristo se moría pronto era cosa indudable: no había más
que verle. ¿Qué iba a ser de ella, privada de la dirección y consejo
de tan excelente hombre? ¡Cuidado que sabía el tal! Toda la
ciencia del mundo la poseía al dedillo, y la naturaleza humana, el
aquel de la vida que para otros es tan difícil de conocer, para él era
como un catecismo que se sabe de memoria. ¡Qué hombre!
(III, iv, 7, p. 343)

More characteristic than the use of direct speech or free indirect
discourse singly is a combination of both of them with narrative.
And narrative in Galdós has its own highly individual stamp since he
is much more thorough-going than most realist novelists in reflecting
subjective values. As Antonio Sánchez Barbudo (*20*) and G. A. and
J. J. Alfieri (*33*) have shown, he allows the rhythm of speech, and
very colloquial speech at that, to permeate his whole narrative
expression, reflecting in his easy, chatty language, even in straight
narrative, the narrator's familiar relationship with his characters
(*29*, p. 296). Galdós's variant of the narrative form conveys familiarity and very often sympathy but by no means identification, for a
strong dose of irony is frequently administered. It is this highly
characteristic mode of narration which enables him to pass so
smoothly from narration to indirect or direct reflexion of the spoken
word. Fortunata's frenzied thoughts when, abandoned by Juanito
(III, iii, 2), she contemplates entering the Santa Cruz's house and
attacking Jacinta are a particularly good example. As the narrator
tells us of Fortunata's intentions, he starts to echo the words of her
own thoughts:

¿Cuál era el intento de Fortunata y qué iba a hacer allí?
¡Friolera! . . . Pues nada más que entrar en la casa, sin pedir
permiso a nadie, llamar, colarse de rondón, dando gritos y atro-
pellando a todo el que encontrara, llegarse a Jacinta, cogerla por
el moño y . . . (III, iii, 2, p. 324)

Subsequently he passes to direct speech, to voice Fortunata's conviction that Jacinta had robbed her of her husband. There follows an
alternation of narrative, free indirect speech and disparaging direct
comment mingled with respect as Estupiñá, Moreno-Isla and finally
Doña Bárbara, Jacinta and one of her sisters are seen to come out.

The varied technique lends flexibility to a scene in which it is essential to convey the emotional stress Fortunata is suffering and yet keep the story moving.

Similarly, Doña Lupe, preoccupied with the scandal Fortunata's baby will produce, is presented, in a mixture of narration and indirect discourse, as almost tempted to commit some of her own money to avoid it:

> Esto no se podría sufrir sin cubrirse de baldón; esto no lo toleraría doña Lupe, aunque tuviera que dar no sólo el dinero ajeno, sino el propio . . . Tanto como el propio, no, vamos; pero, en fin, así lo pensaba para poder expresar de una manera enfática su grandísimo enojo. (IV, iii, 5, p. 473)

She then passes on to the dramatic monologue previously referred to.

Salvador Bacarisse (*34*) has drawn attention to the linguistic technique of the passage in which Fortunata's fatal haemorrhage occurs. The event is captured essentially, with some intertwined narrative fragments, through her immediate sensations and appropriate vocabulary with the deliberate avoidance of conceptual precision ('una cosa extraña', 'algo', 'aquel fenómeno') and the conscious aim, by the use of the imperfect tense, of 'visualizing' the scene.

> . . . la joven sintió dentro de sí una cosa extraña. Se le nublaron los ojos, y se le desprendía algo en su interior como cuando vino al mundo Juan Evaristo; sólo que era sin dolor ninguno. No pudo apreciar bien aquel fenómeno, porque se quedó desvanecida. Al volver en sí advirtió que era ya de día claro . . . Fue a coger a su hijo en brazos y apenas podía con él. Le faltaban las fuerzas, ¡pero de qué manera!, y hasta la vista parecía amenguársele y pervertírsele, porque veía los objetos desfigurados y se equivocaba a cada momento, creyendo ver lo que no existía. Se asustó mucho y llamó; pero nadie vino en su auxilio. Después de llamar como unas tres veces, fue a llamar la cuarta, y . . . aquello sí era grave: no tenía voz, no le sonaba la voz, se le quedaba la intención de la palabra en la garganta sin poderla pronunciar. (IV, vi, 12, p. 536)

We are given the impressions provided by the senses, from which, by a different process, we have to deduce the cause and the facts, and even to rectify what seemed incontrovertible. The narrator tells us that Fortunata called out three times, but as Bacarisse points out (*34*, p. 246), *llamó* is not factual: Fortunata thought she called out but could not.

The tone of the narrative may be coloured by the characters' attitude to the events narrated. The breaking of Maxi's moneybox (II, i, 5) is related in heroic terms (see p. 52). The day of Juanito's desertion of Fortunata is called, with some justification, 'aquel aciago día' (p. 324), and the same term is used, with ironic exaggeration and in a mock-elevated tone, concerning Juan Pablo's failure to obtain a loan from Doña Lupe: 'En la noche de aquel aciago día que creyó deber marcar con la piedra más negra que en su triste camino hubiera . . .' (p. 474). In some instances, Galdós reflects the state of mind of his characters by transferring the physical setting from one place to another. Thus Moreno-Isla '. . . regresaba a su casa de vuelta de un paseíto por Hyde Park . . ., digo, por el Retiro' (IV, ii, 1, p. 445). When Juan Pablo Rubín is raised to unexpected political heights, 'De todos lados de la cámara . . ., digo del café, vino gente a felicitar al gobernador . . .' (IV, v, 6, p. 500). Popular clichés and idioms, exclamations and snatches of conversation are often incrusted into the narrative and are freely combined, as we have seen, with direct speech or free indirect discourse. Thus Doña Isabel Cordero's business sense is reflected in the language applied to the imperative question of marrying off her daughters: 'el trabajo de exhibir y airear el muestrario . . .', 'Era forzoso *hacer el artículo*', 'concurrir con el *género* a tal o cual tertulia de amigas . . .' (I, ii, 7, p. 33). Juan Pablo Rubín's ill-digested philosophy of Nature is expounded in racy narrative form and with evident ironic intention. In particular, he denounces marriage as appropriate only to a primitive stage of society:

> Sólo en la edad pueril, cuando a la sociedad se le cae la baba y vive debajo la férula del dómine, se comprende que exista y tenga prosélitos la institución llamada matrimonio, unión perpetua de los sexos, contraviniendo la ley de Naturaleza . . .   ¿Y a santo de qué? vamos a ver . . . Eso sí, por encima de todo, la Naturaleza. (III, i, 6, p. 306)

Unfortunately, Rubín's audience consists merely of the very ordinary habitués of the café, but as the narrator innocently reminds us Jesus's first disciples were simple illiterate fishermen and street-walkers.

From this same tendency derive the exaggerated titles and epithets lavished on Galdós's personages —'este insigne hijo de Madrid', 'aquel gran filósofo', 'aquella incomparable señora', 'el ilustrado joven', and so on— and the superabundance of nicknames and tags in his prose.

The reiterated use of such expressions as *el Delfín, la mona del cielo, la virgen y fundadora* or *la rata eclesiástica, el basilisco, Rubinius vulgaris* and *Ulmus sylvestris* show Galdós's delight in playing with clichés in order to achieve a remarkable degree of integration between the narrator and his fictional world. The evident pleasure he takes in immersing himself in the commonplace, well documented by Sánchez Barbudo (*20*, pp. 23-30), does not however imply approval. Failure to realize this leads to the common fallacy of some critics, especially the Generation of '98, of equating Galdós's attitude with the attitude and language of his characters. Thus he is condemned by Unamuno as a trite middle-class popularizer ('el estilo de café, el estilo de la improvisación periodística, el estilo parlamentario, el de artículo de fondo')[19] and has the famous nickname 'Don Benito el garbancero' applied to him by one of Valle-Inclán's characters. Today, when the immediate hostile reaction against the society of Restoration Spain which Galdós reflected so faithfully, though not uncritically, is past, we can better appreciate the true measure of his linguistic talents.

Another major question of technique concerns telling as opposed to showing. Since the publication of Percy Lubbock's famous study, with its emphasis on dramatic incidents or scenes, the contrast between the two methods has become one of the commonplaces of criticism of the novel. If displaying characters in action is in general a superior method of presentation to simply narrating their activities, it is also true that some narration is in normal circumstances indispensable and is a more economical means of covering a great deal of ground. As Lubbock says:

> A novelist instinctively sees the chief turns and phases of his story expressed in the form of the thing acted, where narrative ceases and a direct light falls upon his people and their doings. It must be so, for this is the sharpest effect within his range; and the story must naturally have the benefit of it, wherever the emphasis is to fall most strongly ... But precisely because it has this high value it will need to be used prudently ... In the scene, it is clear, there can be no foreshortening of time or space ... and therefore it is, for its length, expensive in the matter of time and space; an oblique narrative will give the effect of further distances

---

[19]'El estilo de Galdós', in 'Alrededor del estilo' (1924), *Obras completas* (Escelicer, 1967), VII, p. 916.

and longer periods with much greater economy.[20]

Galdós, naturally enough, uses both methods, but his practice has some distinctive features; often his procedure lies somewhere in between scene and narrative. To illustrate this, let us look in some detail at the first chapters of the first two parts in which Galdós has to introduce effectively his two principal male personages, Juan Santa Cruz and Maximiliano Rubín.

In the first case, he does this by starting from the time in the 1860s when Villalonga is able to recount stories from his student life and by bringing his portrayal into closer focus once the narrator has met him; he characterizes him briefly by means of his inevitable diminutive, refers to his parents' position and concludes with Juanito's first visit to Paris. The vehicle used is narration but with a marked familiar tone, frequent snatches of reported conversation, exclamations and side-comments. Only after we have a concise but clear sketch of Juanito as an individual are we given, in Chapter II, the long 'vistazo histórico' on Madrid commerce and the Santa Cruz family which explains Juanito's background. This chapter, in turn, gradually builds up to the present, and, going on to consider the related Arnáiz family, ends with a reference to Jacinta's marriage, though postponing discussion of this important event. Chapter III takes us back in time. The story of Estupiñá, bringing together earlier political and commercial threads, is related, in order to prepare the way for the crucial occurrence of the novel, as Galdós's narrator, explicitly and perhaps unnecessarily, reiterates:

> Si Juanito Santa Cruz no hubiera hecho esta visita, esta historia no se habría escrito. Se hubiera escrito otra, eso sí, porque doquiera que el hombre vaya lleva consigo su novela; pero ésta no. (I, iii, 3, p. 40)

This fundamental incident is the first dramatic scene of the novel: the meeting of Juanito with Fortunata, vividly captured both in visual terms and in speech. It is well prepared for by a preliminary narrative passage, in which the poultry and egg shop, at the entrance of La Cava de San Miguel, no. 11, with its implacable slaughter of chickens, is described. Juanito looks in ('lo que es natural', the

---

[20]*The Craft of Fiction* (London, 1921), pp. 267-8. Wayne Booth's reservations (*Rhetoric of Fiction*, p. 8) should however be borne in mind.

narrator adds slyly) at the open door of an apartment and sees there a pretty girl, who is equally curious. She is dressed in typical kerchief and *mantón* and makes a movement which is sharply focussed in the narration and which links her with her surroundings:

> . . . hizo ese característico arqueo de brazos y alzamiento de hombros con que las madrileñas del pueblo se agazapan dentro del mantón, movimiento que les da cierta semejanza con una gallina que esponja su plumaje y se ahueca para volver luego a su volumen natural. (I, iii, 4, p. 41)

Juanito does not let this opportunity pass; he looks her up and down ('al observar lo linda que era y lo bien calzada que estaba') and starts a conversation by asking for Estupiñá. The girl's next two movements, stepping forward and putting her hand to her mouth, encourage him further, and he refuses to be put off by his distaste for the raw egg she is eating. When she offers to share it with him, he reluctantly refuses:

> Por entre los dedos de la chica se escurrían aquellas babas gelatinosas y transparentes. Tuvo tentaciones Juanito de aceptar la oferta; pero no: le repugnaban los huevos crudos.
> —No, gracias.

The contrast between their two worlds could not have been more graphically illustrated.

Two further snippets of information help complete the picture. First, the shrill call of *Fortunaaá* tells us the girl's name. Second, Juanito conscientiously visited Estupiñá every day and, not put off, as the narrator informs us with his tongue in his cheek, by the many stairs, always approached by way of the egg shop in La Cava. His subsequent encounters are obviously going to be more successful.

Chapter IV, entitled 'Perdición y salvamento del Delfín', reveals indirectly Juanito's involvement with Fortunata and, picking up the loose ends of Chapter II, describes the marriage to Jacinta arranged by his mother. On their honeymoon, related in Chapter V, Jacinta wheedles out of her husband the details of his affair with Fortunata; as Suzanne Raphaël has noted (26), Fortunata is the hidden presence throughout the episode. His early relations with the two heroines are thus intertwined with the history of his family and dealt with once and for all, with wealth of detail, in the first five chapters. The pace can now speed up again and a period of months, even years, of apparent family harmony is dispatched in a few lines of narrative at the beginning of Chapter VI.

The presentation of Maxi in Part II is shorter, and contained within the first chapter headed by his name. After a description of his brothers, the narrative begins to centre on him, bringing out first his inadequate physique and indifference to his studies and then factors concerning his manliness (see p. 94). Then the story comes to focus on that winter night of early 1874 when he met Fortunata in the *hotelito* of Olmedo and Feliciana (in the earlier manuscript version he meets her in the street). The encounter is not as developed or dramatic as Juanito's but Maxi's eagerness to gain her favour by telling the time with such pedantic exactness —'Las nueve menos siete minutos . . . y medio' (p. 165)— is well done. While Fortunata's indifference to this 'bicho raro' is related mainly from the outside by the narrator, Maxi is seen from within as his physical and mental lethargy fall off him and he loses his previously inviolate respect —though not yet his fear— for his aunt: 'los antiguos moldes estaban rotos' (p. 168). His emancipation is consummated in the great scene, comic and moving at the same time, when he sets out to break open his own money box (II, i, 5). Not that he has the courage simply to take his money and face Doña Lupe's wrath; under the disrespectful and suspicious eyes of Papitos, he determines to substitute a replica to cover up his action. The stages by which he carries out this undertaking are carefully recorded; Maxi's emotions at the perils involved are reflected subjectively, with the narrator's occasional comments adding to the ironic illusion of a heroic and desperate feat (*14*, pp. 256-7, *17*, pp. 122-3): the difficulty of breaking the earthenware container silently; the explanation given to Papitos for needing the mortar; the noise made by the first frantic blow, so that he decided to break it on the bed; the fact that in his confusion he nearly struck the new box; his fancy that the fragments of red clay on the bed were bloodstains and the ironic equation by the narrator of the whole harmless action with a bloody murder; his excessive haste in putting the small coins into the new money box, so that they block the entrance slit. The following paragraph on his apprehensions shows clearly how the third-person narration is used for subjective effects; the last sentence, a direct comment from the narrator, maintains the ironic tone of high melodrama:

No había tiempo que perder. Sentía pasos. ¿Subiría ya doña
Lupe? No, no era ella; pero pronto vendría y era forzoso despa-
char. Aquellos cascos, ¿dónde los echaría? He aquí un problema
que le puso los pelos de punta al asesino. Lo mejor era envolver
aquellos despojos sangrientos en un pañuelo y tirarlos en medio
de la calle, cuando saliera. ¿Y la sangre? Limpió la colcha como
pudo, soplando el polvo. Después advirtió que su mano derecha y
el puño de la camisa conservaban algunas señales, y se ocupó en
borrarlas cuidadosamente. También la mano del almirez necesitó
de un buen limpión. ¿Tendría algo en la ropa? Se miró de pies a
cabeza. No había nada, absolutamente nada. Como todos los
matadores en igual caso, fue escrupuloso en el examen; pero a
estos desgraciados se les olvida siempre algo, y donde menos lo
piensan se conserva el dato acusador que ilumina a la justicia.
(pp. 170-1)

How subjective individual judgements can be even on matters of
physical fact is shown by the question of the similarity between the
two money boxes. When he bought the replica, he compared the
two and was quite satisfied that they were identical. Once he has
broken the old one, though, he is struck by apprehensions that they
are very different, and launches forth into short inner monologues
about the consequences. For a moment he takes courage and
contemplates asserting his undoubted right to the money, but
speedily thinks better of it. Then he fears that Doña Lupe will come
across pieces of the old money box when she sweeps the floor, or
find out that he had changed money at the shop or simply read his
guilty secret in his face. But Doña Lupe's scrutiny is this time
concerned with his medical condition, and after taking enormous
care to prevent the money rattling in his pocket, he is able to carry
out, in the next chapter, his scheme to set up Fortunata in a modest
flat.

Other important scenes concern the violent encounters of the
male and female protagonists, Juanito and Maxi and Fortunata and
Jacinta. The latter encounter will be considered later, as an essential
part of a complex structural pattern. The first case serves as a good
example of the blending of narrative and scene. Three stages can be
discerned in the episode. First, when Maxi's suspicions regarding his
wife are confirmed by a friend (II, vii, 9), the narrator describes how
he returns home and then sets out again to watch the houses he
suspects may harbour the lovers. The narration is permeated with

his emotions, though these are not presented directly. His self-reproach at having allowed Fortunata to take his revolver from him is expressed in free indirect speech: ' ¡Qué tonto estuvo él en permitírselo!' (p. 285). He is anxious for the truth and terrified by the prospect of it, and he notes poignantly the mechanical *noria* or wind pump outside Las Micaelas which had corresponded to his emotions while Fortunata was in the convent. When its wind-wheel was functioning it served as encouragement to him, but when it was motionless it induced a feeling of despair: 'El estar parado el motor parecíale señal de desventura' (II, v, 3, p. 232). Now it has stopped. In this economical way Galdós is referring back to the previous episode, thus closing the cycle of Maxi's illusions initiated at Las Micaelas. In his agony Maxi wishes the night would descend and blot out the sight of the *noria*, 'que le parecía el ojo del bufón testigo, expresando todo el sarcasmo del mundo' (p. 285). These thoughts are clearly Maxi's, but the narrator also continues to describe from outside:

> Maldición sacrílega escapóse de sus labios y renegó de que hubieran venido a estar tan cerca su deshonra y el santuario donde le habían dorado la infame píldora de su ilusión. En otros términos: él había ido allí en busca de una hostia y le habían dado una rueda de molino ... Y lo peor era que se la había tragado.

Why this explicit intrusion of the narrator, with its melodramatic tone, its contrived metaphor, its play on words? It might be thought to mar a scene better left to produce its effect by itself. Yet it is important to see why Galdós has used this device; he wishes to stress particularly by these ironic exaggerations the extent of the universal despair experienced by Maxi, the complete impossibility of escape from the situation of which he feels himself to be the victim.

The second stage begins with the arrival of Juanito Santa Cruz and the subsequent brawl; narrative and direct speech are adroitly combined. The narrator interprets for us Juanito's fairly obvious thoughts and motives: the 'misteriosa aprensión, la conciencia tal vez' as he guesses who is approaching him, the proud reaction with immediate violence, the calculating realization that he could easily kill his puny opponent whom he treats in word and deed as an insignificant insect ('escuerzo', 'cucaracha', 'te digo que te pateo'). Maxi's frantic denunciations are also given in direct speech (' ¡Canalla!;

¡Indecente!'; 'Te voy a matar'; ' ¡Ladrón, ratero . . !'; ' ¡Ladrón . . ., asesino!'), but his desperate struggle is conveyed in narrative which at times directly echoes Maxi's thoughts ('¿Dónde está la justicia? ¿Dónde está la vindicta del débil?', p. 286).

The third stage reveals, mainly in direct speech, the varied mistaken and unsympathetic attitudes taken by other people. The first man comes up only after he is sure Maxi is not fatally wounded and thinks he is an old man. Misled by Maxi's voice which in his more and more inarticulate outbursts of fury has become shrill and unmanly, the group that gathers around concludes that he is a pansy and becomes curious:

> —*Sobrevino* una pendencia.
> —No, cuestión de faldas, ¿verdad?
> — ¡Quita allá! Pero ¿no ves que es marica?
> Las mujeres le miraban con más interés.

To make matters worse, the police treat him roughly as a ruffian. All sectors of society deal with the poor victim with marked lack of comprehension or respect: 'todo el sarcasmo del mundo' is demonstrated in practice.

IV Depiction of society

We have noted that the coverage of society in this novel, as in any other, is necessarily selective and incomplete. *Fortunata y Jacinta* does, however, set out to cover certain areas in great depth. The starting point and the hub of the narration are the business activities, great and small, of the capital: from these stem the sort of lives the individual characters lead. The world of finance and large-scale commerce is described in detail in the first part. It is noteworthy that there is no attempt to bring in manufacture or production: no factory, no managers, no workmen fall within its scope; the emphasis is primarily on distribution, consumption, the economics of buying and selling, and of lending and borrowing. To a large extent, this is a result of the setting in Madrid, predominantly an administrative and consumer-service city. That Galdós is not unaware of industrial problems is shown in the brief but significant visit the young Santa Cruz couple pay to a factory in Barcelona during their honeymoon (I, v, 3). The rest of the route taken during the honeymoon, first through Burgos and Saragossa and then via Valencia to Seville, also serves to indicate that Madrid is not all Spain. The friendly debates between Don Baldomero and Arnáiz on protection and free trade (I, ii, 1) ventilate an important economic issue (see *1*, pp. 277-81).

The development of the Santa Cruz family is most carefully documented. As a new aristocracy of wealth, it is treated quite explicitly as a dynasty, with quasi-regal deference. Don Baldomero I is succeeded by Don Baldomero II and the heir-apparent Juanito is consistently called *el Delfín*, employing the title of the French crown prince. Yet it has been pointed out that the patronymic Santa Cruz has the ring of a *converso*, or converted Jewish, name, which would be quite consistent with commercial activity. The first Baldomero had been a simple *hortera* or shop assistant, who steadily worked his way up, imposing a rigid discipline upon his employees and family alike. And his son was so socially limited in his youth that Barbarita was seriously alarmed at the prospect of marrying him. By this arranged marriage, however, two commercial families, Santa Cruz and Arnáiz, already remotely connected, are brought together.

When Don Baldomero II retired to make way for innovations (in that year of change, 1868), he left the shop in the hands not of his son and heir Juanito, but of 'los chicos', relatives of his wife and himself respectively. The business stays in the family, but the direct descendant is no longer a tradesman, however exalted, but a gentleman of leisure. The evolution over three generations is clear: self-made man, prosperous business man, idle inheritor. Their success-story epitomizes the rise of the commercial middle class to affluence and power. Juanito's university education, easy sophistication and life of ease from birth contrasts markedly with his father's initial lack of social graces, limited horizons and years of hard work. For his part, Don Baldomero delights in his son's very different life-style: this, according to Santa Cruz senior, is called progress. It is a case no longer of *nouveaux riches*, but of a new aristocracy.

For her part, Barbarita Arnáiz had grown up equally in a world of shop-keepers, with the smell of sandalwood in her nostrils; she continues to display commercial values all her life by her delight in shopping. The marriage she planned between her only son and her niece Jacinta consolidates the bonds between the two families and of course increases the in-breeding. It is evident that Jacinta's barrenness —in sharp contrast with the embarrassing fertility of Jacinta's parents and sisters— is intended to symbolize the in-bred nature of the new ruling class.

The Santa Cruz and Arnáiz families represent, however, only part of the proliferation of intertwining relationships in the commercial development of Madrid from the beginning of the nineteenth century. Galdós rehearses in a leisurely fashion and with evident delight the transformations in materials, design, and fashion in the drapery business as home-produced goods give way to Oriental imports (the rise and fall of the colourful *mantón de Manila*, now the preserve of the *pueblo*, is significant, I, ii, 5, p. 29), to be succeeded in turn, in the railway age, by European products. As trade alters so the fortunes of families and individuals from various parts of Spain change. The wives of the first of both the Santa Cruz and the Arnáiz dynasties were descended from one Matías Trujillo, a packsaddle maker from Extremadura, and there are many other Trujillos to be found. The Bonilla family came from Cadiz and the Morenos from the Valle de Mena (Province of Burgos): the latter in particular proliferate, to such an extent that the narrator abandons hope of tracing all their relationships. What in fact fascinates Galdós most is the constantly shifting position of wealth and power. He is particularly concerned with the mingling of social classes these changes bring about, and the varying relationship thus existing between distinct sections of the middle classes. Thus there are rich Morenos —like the banker Manuel Moreno-Isla, Doña Guillermina's nephew— and poor Morenos —like Doña Casta. She is a member by marriage of the no less numerous Samaniego family which never manages to prosper, but maintains various contacts with its more well-to-do counterparts and relatives (Jacinta's elder sister Candelaria married a Samaniego) in the course of the story. Similarly, we can see in Estupiñá an example of business failure, through his irrepressible urge for conversation, so that he is reduced to the rôle of little more than an old retainer to the Santa Cruz family. By contrast, the more prosperous members of the commercial middle classes effect unions with the impoverished aristocracy. Thus a brother of the Duque de Gravelinas married a Moreno and of this marriage Guillermina Pacheco was born; and the Duque himself married one of the daughters of a wealthy business man, the marqués de Casarredonda. 'Ya tenemos' —the narrator comments— 'aquí perfectamente enganchados a la aristocracia antigua y el comercio moderno' (I, vi, 2, p. 66).

The new aristocracy of wealth, which is to find its political form with the Restoration, can be seen to be spreading outward into every influential aspect of life (see *38*, p. 20). Galdós pinpoints this representational quality in the list of guests at the Santa Cruz's Christmas Eve dinner in 1873 even though he ends on a rather burlesque note at the expense of Federico Ruiz and Estupiñá:

Veinticinco personas había en la mesa, siendo de notar que el conjunto de los convidados ofrecía perfecto muestrario de todas las clases sociales. La enredadera de que antes hablé había llevado allí sus vástagos más diversos. Estaba el marqués de Casa-Muñoz, de la aristocracia monetaria, y un Alvarez de Toledo, hermano del duque de Gravelinas, de la aristocracia antigua, casado con una Trujillo. Resultaba no sé qué irónica armonía de la conjunción aquella de los dos nobles, oriundo el uno del gran Alba y el otro sucesor de don Pascual Muñoz, dignísimo ferretero de la calle de Tintoreros. Por otro lado nos encontramos con Samaniego, que era casi un hortera, muy cerca de Ruiz-Ochoa, o sea la alta Banca.

Villalonga representaba el Parlamento: Aparisi, el Municipio; Joaquín Pez, el Foro, y Federico Ruiz representaba muchas cosas a la vez: la Prensa, las Letras, la Filosofía, la Crítica musical, el Cuerpo de Bomberos, las Sociedades Económicas, la Arqueología y los Abonos químicos. Y Estupiñá, con su levita negra de paño fino, ¿qué representaba? El comercio antiguo, sin duda; las tradiciones de la calle de Postas, el contrabando, quizá *la religión de nuestros mayores*, por ser hombre tan sinceramente piadoso. (I, x, 5, p. 138)

Other types of diversification of activity are indicated too. International contacts have made Moreno-Isla into an Anglophile contemptuous of all things Spanish. Doña Guillermina finds her own personal satisfaction in charitable works. Even Juanito toys momentarily with the idea of scholarship, but quickly abandons it. Nor will he have any truck with finance or with politics, in which his friend Villalonga has made such a success. He represents, as we shall see, yet another option of the second-generation capitalist: opting out of an active existence, living as a *señorito*.

'Perfecto muestrario de *todas* las clases sociales' states the passage I have just quoted. This is evidently far from being the case. In another much-quoted passage, the narrator makes some confident declarations about society in a manner which appears extremely superficial and complacent:

Es curioso observar cómo nuestra edad, por otros conceptos infeliz, nos presenta una dichosa confusión de todas las clases, mejor dicho, la concordia y reconciliación de todas ellas . . . Aquí se ha resuelto el problema sencilla y pacíficamente, gracias al temple democrático de los españoles y a la escasa vehemencia de las preocupaciones nobiliarias . . . han salido amigos el noble tronado y el plebeyo ensoberbecido por un título universitario; y de amigos, pronto han pasado a parientes. Esta confusión es un bien, y gracias a ella no nos aterra el contagio de la guerra social, porque tenemos ya en la masa de la sangre un socialismo atenuado e inofensivo.

He goes on to say that the only differences now existing between individuals are innate differences of intelligence. Nevertheless one class difference remains, money:

La otra determinación positiva de clases, el dinero, está fundada en principios económicos tan inmutables como las leyes físicas, y querer impedirla viene a ser lo mismo que intentar beberse la mar. (I, vi, 1, pp. 65-6)

What are we to make of what seems to be a travesty of Spanish social history a hundred years ago? First, it is important to understand that Galdós is concerned here with questions of noble rank, not with social justice: by 'plebeian' he means a man of humble birth, like Baldomero I, Casarredonda or Matías Trujillo, who has been able to pull himself up in the world by his own bootstraps. Galdós is referring in this context to the new impelling economic forces of entrepreneurial capitalism which produce rises and falls of fortunes seldom envisaged in earlier times. His portrayal of society, therefore, stands or falls by the accuracy with which he presents the class in which most of the shifts of power occur. For this reason Antonio Regalado García is making the wrong demands on the novelist when he accuses him of a complacent acquiescence in an unjust society:

> Toda la obra de Galdós está orientada en favor del *Statu quo* de la Restauración y contra los dos mayores peligros que lo amenazaban, la revolución política y el cambio de la estructura social propugnada por las aspiraciones del cuarto estado, encarnadas en la ideología de socialistas y anarquistas. (*3*, p. 193)

As Peter Goldman has pointed out in his criticism of Regalado's book (pp. 113-17), the strength of working-class organization was not such as to warrant the attention here demanded. Nor can Galdós, from the evidence of the novel, be labelled unequivocally either a supporter or an opponent of the status quo. Other critics, like John Sinnigen and Julio Rodríguez Puértolas, no less Marxist in orientation, are more perceptive in finding in *Fortunata* 'a comprehensive bourgeois consciousness' (*39*, p. 56), together with a more or less thoroughgoing criticism of bourgeois values (*38*, pp. 13-58 and 92) which does not however threaten its bases (*39*, p. 66). This I would accept as largely true, provided that it is recognized that these criticisms do not constitute anything approaching a view of society as a class-struggle. In my opinion it is more a question of a remarkably clear vision of human failings in a given social context than of any clearly defined political stance.

Various minor touches reinforce the somewhat critical approach towards certain middle-class attitudes. First, there is a remark, reliable or not, made by Doña Manolita Reoyos and incorporated into the narrative. Her presence, as a '*señora* en regla', among the *filomenas* of Las Micaelas to expiate her sins is in itself significant. She makes the following devastating comment on the morals of the aristocratic ladies who visit the Convent:

> . . . toda aquella muchedumbre elegante, libre, en la cual había algunas, justo es decirlo, que habían pecado mucho más, pero muchísimo más que la peor de las que allí estaban encerradas. (II, vi, 5, p. 243)

Less far-reaching are two examples of slight lack of consideration. When Jacinta collects Juanín, fully expecting to adopt him, she clearly loses interest in Adoración:

> —No me olvidaré de ti, Adoración— le dijo la señorita, que con esta frase parecía anunciar que no volvería pronto. (I, x, 3, p. 133)

Then there is Moreno-Isla's condescension to Estupiñá. After they have exchanged an *abrazo*, the Anglophile replies to him 'con la benevolencia un tanto fría que saben emplear los superiores bien educados' (III, ii, 4, p. 318).

There remains, however, the manifestly misleading idea of the 'dichosa reconciliación de todas las clases'. Ricardo Gullón (*31*, pp. 184-6) suggests that a contradiction exists between 'el Galdós teorizante' and 'el Galdós novelador', similar to that discussed by Lukács in the case of Balzac.[21] This is certainly possible, but in my view the explanation lies in the narrative method previously described and the structural pattern of the novel. This excessively complacent tone emanates from the same narrator who is putting such an optimistic gloss on the private lives of the Santa Cruz family. Moreover, up and beyond this point we have viewed society entirely from the point of view of the opulent bourgeoisie. Only later, with the visit to the 'Cuarto Estado', does the wretched existence led by the poor stand revealed in all its horror.

That the new social determinant is money is, undoubtedly, a true enough statement, attested throughout the book. Galdós systematically records the financial position of his characters: Don Baldomero has an annual income of 25,000 *duros*;[22] Barbarita receives from him *mil duretes* a month, and Juanito an allowance of 2,000 *duros*

---

[21]*Studies in European Realism* (London, 1950), Chapters 1-3.

[22]A *duro* (*peso*) = 5 *pesetas;* a *peseta* = 4 *reales*. A *duro* at the time of the Restoration was worth approximately five shillings.

from his father, plus two or three thousand *reales* a month from his mother (I, vi, 3, pp. 68-9). Doña Lupe has a capital of 10,000 *duros* (II, iii, 5, p. 204). By contrast, Severiana's husband is fortunate to earn 14 *reales* a day (I, ix, 8, p. 120) and Nicanora, Ido's wife, gets a *real* per ream of mourning paper, making six or seven *reales* a day (I, ix, 2, p. 104). The contrasts speak for themselves.

A particularly blatant example of how money talks is the negotiation to acquire *el Pitusín*; Guillermina remarks 'es muy caro el animalito', Bárbara is madly curious about 'aquella alhaja que su hija le había comprado: un nieto'; Juanito brutally retorts to his wife: 'Como te ha costado tu dinero'. As James Whiston observes, 'Juanín . . . is degraded and treated as an object of trade' (*35*, p. 85). Likewise, the various political crises of the time are constantly judged in the Santa Cruz circle by their effects on stocks and shares (I, vii, 3, p. 81; I, viii, 3, p. 89; I, xi, 1, p. 151). Whether or not the laws governing economic developments are as rigid, unchangeable and even by implication desirable as the narrator affirms, and whether Galdós himself thought them to be so, need not concern us. It is a view typical of the age and a satisfactory working hypothesis for the purposes of the story. What is more important is that he has presented from inside, as it were, without any misgivings, a very plausible picture of the evolution of capitalist society.

The lower middle-class world of Doña Lupe Rubín, *viuda de* Jáuregui, described in Part II, is very different, though it is even more obviously dominated by money, jubilantly and vulgarly termed *guano* by Torquemada and herself. Doña Lupe is one of those who have moved up in the world. Left a widow in straitened circumstances, she went in for money-lending as an associate of the notorious Torquemada; it brought her prosperity which enabled her to provide for her three nephews, and she became as dedicated to her unsavoury occupation as she was ruthless in exercising it. In a masterly fashion, Galdós represents physically the two sides of her personality, the woman and the money-lender. She has had one breast removed in an operation, so that 'sólo la mitad de su seno era de carne; la otra mitad era insensible, y bien se le podía clavar un puñal sin que le doliese. Lo mismo era su corazón: la mitad de carne, la mitad de algodón' (II, iii, 5, p. 203). Dominated by money considerations down to the smallest details (examples will be given later, p. 75), she also aspires to enter the world of genteel ladies of charity represented by Doña Guillermina. Torquemada, for his part, is a supreme example of the self-made man, the modern capitalist and entrepreneur who is to break decisively if reluctantly into high society in later novels. Typically enough, it is Doña Lupe who, on her deathbed, in *Torquemada en la cruz*, encourages her old friend and partner to marry into the aristocracy. The wealth accumulated in even such sordid activities as usury is not to be gainsaid in this new social setup in which money is practically the only determinant.

The careers of the three Rubín brothers show the varied opportunities open to the petty bourgeoisie. One of them, Nicolás, becomes a priest and is the principal representative, though by no means a worthy one, of the Catholic Church. Galdós's portrayal of him is the harshest in the novel, and also the most explicit; he is depicted as repulsively hairy and uncouth, gluttonous, arrogant and ambitious. Lacking all psychological penetration, he sets out to guide Fortunata and is responsible for her confinement in Las Micaelas; he is a friend of the huge insensitive chaplain of that institution, Don León Pintado. He counsels his brother Juan Pablo to join the Carlists, and is a companion of the group of discontented priests without a living —*Pater*, Quevedo and Pedernero— who meet in the café and dispute with Juan Pablo (II, i, 4). Such dispossessed clerics were an acute problem in nineteenth-century Madrid; one of them, Galeote, was the assassin of the Bishop of Madrid, Martínez Izquierdo, in 1886; Galdós was fascinated by the case and visited Galeote in prison (*6*, p. 107). Father Rubín, for his part, ends up with the quite undeserved distinction of being made a canon.

Quite a lot of space is devoted to the religious development in the Northern suburbs of Madrid. After discussing the hideous architecture inspired by modern French religious establishments, Galdós passes to the spartan building of Las Micaelas where the poor quality of the music matched the ugliness of the structure and the pictures. As the brick-built church grows it gradually blots out the view of the horizon (II, v, 3). The nuns it shelters are similarly limited; they are for the most part authoritarian, fanatical about cleanliness or sentimentally devout; only the stunted and deformed Sor Marcela has any sense of compassion or capacity for giving guidance. The picture of the Church Galdós gives is a bleak rather than a hostile one; it simply does not measure up to the problems posed by society.

The career chosen for the youngest Rubín, Maxi, is the practical and commercial one of pharmacy. The world in which the Rubíns revolve is of small shopkeepers and chemists, of Segismundo Ballester, of *Doña Desdémona* and *las Samaniegas*, Doña Casta Moreno and her daughters. The latter, of course, form one of many links, open or concealed, with the world of the Santa Cruz's: Casta was Barbarita's childhood friend, Aurora was formerly the mistress of Moreno-Isla and is later Juanito's secret lover.

Juan Pablo Rubín introduces us to another aspect of lower middle-class society: the world of café life, political disputes and administrative pretensions. He becomes successively a commercial traveller, a bureaucrat and that typical phenomenon of nineteenth-century Spain, the *cesante* or redundant civil servant. After he has abandoned the Carlists he is eventually incorporated into the administrative world once more by the Restoration. His café companions include other unemployed functionaries like the pompous and vacuous intriguer Basilio Andrés de la Caña, Villaamil, the eternally unfortunate *cesante*, protagonist of *Miau*, and the dispossessed priests mentioned before.

Even in the café society, there is a certain hierarchy (III, i, 2), and the retired colonel Feijoo is in its upper reaches, even though he does not presume to dominate. Independent in means and attitudes, he has close contacts both with the Rubín family and with Villalonga, on the margins of the Santa Cruz circle; he is in a position to recommend his friends, and to make loans when needed.

The working class, though by no means absent from *Fortunata y Jacinta*, is not presented in detail as a coherent entity as the upper and lower middle classes are. It is viewed, initially at any rate, with benevolent condescension through bourgeois eyes when Jacinta and Guillermina penetrate the 'Cuarto Estado' in search of *el Pitusín*; Jacinta's bustle attracts ribald attention. In this detailed description (I, ix), however, the reader is in a position to see beyond the middle-class vision of the two ladies and appreciate the reality of the squalor and wretchedness in the slums. Galdós's awareness of the problem is clearly shown in his article 'La cuestión social' of 1885, quoted by Goldman (*3* (review), p. 116). As they make their slow progress through the streets and then along the tenement corridors, they meet teeming masses of people, especially children, and see no fewer than three youngsters who have died. There are all types: studious, idle, bossy, insolent; some are playing with mud, others have made up their faces like savages. One part of the building, where the Idos live, is especially repulsive:

> . . . el revoco se caía a pedazos, y los rasguños trazados con un clavo en las paredes parecían hechos con más saña; los versos escritos con lápiz en algunas puertas, más necios y groseros; las maderas, más despintadas y roñosas; el aire, más viciado; el vaho que salía por puertas y ventanas, más espeso y repugnante. (I, ix, 2, p. 102)

Even the Mira el Río tenement has its hierarchy, or *capas*, too. At the top of the scale is Severiana, an example of the poor who strive to better themselves. Respectable and thrifty, with a steady husband and a well-kept flat, she is favoured by Doña Guillermina and agrees to take in the dying Mauricia. The latter's exquisite daughter, Adoración, adopted by Severiana, is, thanks to Jacinta's protection, well on her way to assimilation into the lower reaches of the middle class. By contrast, José Ido del Sagrario, despite his educational attainments, lives, in the absolute squalor outlined above, on the miserable earnings of his wife's work in making mourning paper. The Izquierdos, Segunda and José, simply look to the opulent middle class for what they can get out of it. According to Juanito, typical of the prejudices of his class: 'El pueblo no conoce la dignidad. Sólo le mueven sus pasiones o el interés' (I, v, 3, p. 53). Translated into more neutral terms: it is less concerned with social standing and shows its feelings more openly, whether these are of love (Fortunata) or financial advantage (the poor inhabitants of Mira el Río). Segunda, who with her *picador* lover had striven to exploit Fortunata's initial affair with Juanito, later hopes, most unrealistically, for untold advantages through Fortunata's baby and its connexion with the Santa Cruz's; she is frantically indignant when Estupiñá, on the mother's instructions, takes the baby away. José Izquierdo un-successfully plays the confidence trick on Jacinta concerning *el Pitusín*'s parentage and is eventually provided with a new status and livelihood, on Guillermina's recommendation, to serve as an artists' model.

There remain the two most important representatives of the *pueblo*, Mauricia *la dura* and Fortunata. It is worth noticing that Mauricia is the sister of Severiana, the most conspicuous representative of the deserving poor; both can count on Guillermina's protection since their mother was laundress in her parents' house. Moreover, by her work as a *corredora* for Doña Lupe she could undoubtedly have improved her lot had she led a regular life. Her descent into prostitution, alcoholism and rebellion is not explained, but she is very conscious of the oppression of the poor by the rich — 'la pobre siempre debajo y las ricas pateándote la cara' (III, xi, 4, p. 379). Altogether, she is an extreme case of the capacity for gross violence in word and deed possessed, as Galdós sees it, by the people. It is a quality which Fortunata shares to a lesser degree in extreme situations.

The supreme representative of the people is of course Fortunata (see *19*, pp. 23-45). Stephen Gilman has drawn attention to the lack of background provided for her compared with the lavishly detailed environment in which Juanito grows up; he concludes that she is 'sheer human raw material . . . the sculptress of herself', and in an intriguing but unconvincing argument gives her a mythological interpretation, as a bird-like creature hatched from the egg she holds in her hand when we first meet her and converted finally into an angel (*40*, pp. 75-80). In a spirited reply, Carlos Blanco-Aguinaga has rightly emphasized that 'Fortunata, simply, belongs to the "cuarto estado" and, like everybody else in it, she is socially speaking an "orphan"' (*36*, p. 18). We do not know when she was born and her surname is never openly stated, though since José Izquierdo is her paternal uncle, it must (if she is legitimate) be Izquierdo. Among the very meagre facts gleaned from her conversations with Maxi, we learn that her father was a stall-holder in the Plaza Mayor, and an 'hombre honrado' (II, ii, 2, p. 174); she was left an orphan when she was twelve. Her family history is limited to this: not even her parents' names are given. What is constantly emphasized are her characteristic features as a Madrid girl of the people. Her first appearance (I, iii, 4, p. 41), as we have seen (p. 51), bears this out forcibly, as do the terms (*pitusa, nena, chulita, prójima*) applied to her. In language, too, as in taste in food, liking for physical work and impatience with book learning, she is genuinely *pueblo*. The initial attraction she exercises over Juanito brings with it a short-lived period as a *flamenco* dandy (I, iv, 1, p. 42) while Feijoo is completely bowled over by her qualities as an unspoilt working-class *madrileña*. She is semi-literate and extraordinarily ignorant of matters of common knowledge, and Galdós has refrained from making her intelligent or quick to learn; under Maxi's tuition only questions of social etiquette come reasonably easily to her. On the contrary she clings to her own ways and takes pride in her working-class qualities when in difficulty or distress. Both in Las Micaelas and later in the agony produced by Juanito's second desertion, she takes comfort in rough manual work. During Mauricia's illness she delights in making breakfast for Severiana's husband. Like Mauricia, in moments of extreme anger or stress, as in the confrontations with Jacinta (III, vi, 5; III, vii, 3) or the assault on Aurora (IV, vi, 6), she resorts to instinctive violence, to what the narrator calls 'la ira, la pasión y la grosería del pueblo' (p. 408).

Yet this representative of the *pueblo* is transformed in certain respects. She pursues persistently her 'manía de imitación' of Jacinta and her urge towards social respectability ('ser honrada') and to a degree, despite relapses, she succeeds in becoming a lady; accepted as a member of the Rubín family, she mixes socially with the *Samaniegas*; at Severiana's house, when Mauricia is dying, she is not allowed to sweep the floor (III, vi, 5, p. 382). And when she returns to La Cava to have her baby, she is very aware of the difference in her attitude and her aspirations: 'algo se me ha pegado el señorío' (IV, iii, 7, p. 477), she says herself, and the narrator amplifies:

> Indudablemente, la joven se había adecentado mucho y adquirido hábitos de señora, porque la vivienda aquella se le representaba inferior a su categoría, a sus hábitos y a sus gustos.

The ease with which she is accepted socially by the middle class is quite remarkable. The strenuous objections made initially by Maxi's family are on moral not social grounds. This lack of opposition, which stretches credibility to breaking point, indicates the absence of any sense of class conflict in Galdós's world, as the passage quoted earlier (p. 60 makes clear. If the 'dichosa confusión de todas las clases [sociales]' is far from being a reality, Galdós sees no real incompatibility other than financial ones between the classes and hence no question of wholesale class struggle. It is worth noticing that revolutionary impulses in Galdós's novel spring from unbearable individual frustrations, not from class-consciousness. Apart from Mauricia's and Fortunata's rebellious outbursts, the main examples are Juan Pablo Rubín and Izquierdo. The former, beset by debts, denounces private property, the Pope and the Monarchy and advocates free love, undermining the very bulwarks of the State. The narrator comments:

> ¿Y qué menos podía hacer el desgraciado Rubín que descargar contra el orden social y los poderes históricos la horrible angustia que llenaba su alma? (IV, v, 4, p. 495)

Once, however, he is given a post well beyond his expectations or deserts, he assumes a haughty dignity of manner and casts off his mistress, the unfortunate Refugio. Even the apparently revolutionary claims of Izquierdo are highly personal; they arise more from a chronic inferiority complex about his illiteracy than from genuine political beliefs and are not socially or economically oriented in a class-conscious fashion.

For Galdós, then, wealth, not class, now determines the make-up of society. Some, as we have seen, have risen from plebeian stock, others, having advanced some way on the social scale, are determined to progress further. Doña Lupe is a typical example, and it is no coincidence that members of her circle of acquaintances are among those rising fastest, by good connexions or by ruthlessness. Torquemada, Juan Pablo, Nicolás and Aurora are obvious examples. Others, like Estupiñá, Doña Casta and José Ido, have fallen back, and a person like Ballester, as a result of his loyalty, seems likely to join them.

In its increasing prosperity the middle class tends to become internationalized and detached from its origins (the comparison of Juanito with his father illustrates this, as does the case of Moreno-Isla). The *pueblo*, on the other hand, is seen as the primitive repository of truth and authenticity. Admittedly, this view is expressed in a distinctly patronizing way by various middle-class characters like Juanito and Doña Guillermina or, as in the following passage, by the narrator:

> El pueblo, en nuestras sociedades, conserva las ideas y los sentimientos elementales en su tosca plenitud, como la cantera contiene el mármol, materia de la forma. El pueblo posee las

verdades grandes y en bloque, y a él acude la civilización conforme se le van gastando las menudas, de que vive. (III, vii, 3, p. 407)

We have no reason to doubt that Galdós shared this basic concept, although he has expressed it in the condescending tone of the middle-class society he is presenting so faithfully. The most obvious and significant instance in which the 'tosca plenitud' of the *pueblo* supplies the 'civilización gastada' of the in-bred bourgeoisie with new life from the unspoilt quarry of the common people is Fortunata's baby. For the moment it is sufficient to note that this important event produces, not any benefit for the people, but renewal for the middle class, among whom it causes, as Sinnigen points out, a certain heightened awareness: it is redemption not revolution (*39*, p. 66). Galdós's aspiration would appear to be the gradual assimilation of the *pueblo* into an enlightened and self-renewing middle class, not a confrontation between them. As Goldman, drawing on other evidence, has put it, 'If stability was for Galdós the prerequisite of progress, conciliation was its by-word' (*5*, p. 82).

V Portrayal of minor characters

Novelists manipulating a large number of characters have to find some way of fixing them as recognizable beings in their readers' minds. This is especially the case with minor functional characters who are not granted an extended period of development: a kind of shorthand is needed to produce rapid type-casting on demand. The devices adopted to ensure it are varied. At its most simple the name of the character may be relevant, as appropriate or ironically incongruous: José Ido del Sagrario's name implies colloquially that he is crazy; Torquemada's brings in inquisitorial associations; Don Baldomero's links him with General Espartero, also a Don Baldomero; the doctor Francisco de Quevedo is as dull as his famous namesake was witty. As well as the tags like *El delfín* and *Rubinius vulgaris*, already discussed (p. 49), distinctive labels are frequently attached to the characters; Doña Lupe *la de los pavos*, Mauricia *la dura*, *Doña Desdémona*. The most amusing, perhaps, is Izquierdo's nickname *Platón*, given him not in commemoration of the philosopher, but because of the size of the plate he used. The character may be given special physical qualities, with some distinctive features, or some oddity accentuated to make it memorable. Dickens excels in, and abuses, this sort of portrayal. Galdós uses physical description for this purpose in moderation and without exaggeration; Nicolás Rubín is characterized by his excess of hair; Doña Lupe's appearance is described mischievously in Cervantine fashion with apparent praise and just a little too much telling detail:

> Sobre el labio superior, fino y violado cual los bordes de una reciente herida, le corría un bozo tenue, muy tenue, como el de los chicos precoces, vello finísimo que no la afeaba ciertamente; por el contrario, era quizás la única pincelada feliz de aquel rostro semejante a las pinturas de la Edad Media, y hacía la gracia el tal bozo de ir a terminarse sobre el pico derecho de la boca con una verruguita muy mona, de la cual salían dos o tres pelos bermejos que a la luz brillaban retorcidos como hilillos de cobre. (II, iii, 3, p. 199)

For her part, Doña Guillermina has a distinctive roguish blinking of the eyes. *Doña Desdémona*'s immense girth and her picturesque (and functional) aviary serve to fix her in our memory.

Other obvious examples of distinctive physical description are
Torquemada and José Ido. Torquemada is described in terms of his
half-military, half-ecclesiastical appearance, the seldom-changed
collar of his shirt (on his first appearance, II, iii, 1, it is 'casi limpio'
because it is Sunday), his trousers which rise far too high up his legs
(on a later occasion, it is said that *el difunto era más chico*) and his
squeaky boots. Ido, who recurs in no fewer than eight works with
more or less identical traits (*22*), borders on caricature, with his
'cara enfermiza y toda llena de lóbulos y carúnculas; los pelos
bermejos y muy tiesos, como crines de escobillón' (I, viii, 3, p. 90),
and 'lo desengoznado de su cuerpo, la escualidez carunculosa de su
cara y el desarrollo cada vez mayor de la nuez' (III, vi, 2, p. 372),
especially when *se electriza* on eating meat:

> le temblaba horriblemente el párpado, y . . . las carúnculas del
> cuello y los berrugones de la cara, inyectados y turgentes, pare-
> cían próximos a reventar. (I, ix, 6, p. 111)

More frequently, however, Galdós adopts a characteristic technique of making his creations resemble some recognizable object of
reference outside themselves: an animal, a well-known historical
figure, a famous painting, etc. Thus the bluff Don Baldomero looks
like a Newfoundland dog, and Quevedo like an alligator. Estupiñá
resembles a parrot as well as Rossini and Basilio Andrés de la Caña
the Italian statesman Cavour. Villaamil is like the recently-discovered
mummy Rameses II. When José Ido has one of his attacks his wife
Nicanor resembles, in his eyes at least, the Venus of Medici. The
most developed example of this technique is Mauricia *la dura*, whose
physical likeness to Napoleon, as reflected in specific paintings and
engravings, is noted on several occasions as she sinks from the youth-
ful exuberance of looking like the First Consul to the decaying
angular aspect of the ex-Emperor at St Helena.

Speech habits, always important in Galdós, have a definite rôle in
this technique of rapid characterization in the use of specific identification tags or *muletillas* of the 'I shall never leave Mr Micawber'
type. Galdós is a rich supplier of *muletillas* (see Chamberlin, *10*).
Examples in the novel are Torquemada's '¿Y la familia?', Doña
Lupe's 'detenidamente' and 'en toda la extensión de la palabra',
Ido's 'naturalmente' and Nicolás's 'Esta es la cosa' (this last example
is added late, in galley-proof). The vacuous rhetorical rivalry of the

Marqués de Casa-Muñoz and Aparisi gives rise to a good deal of linguistic humour. Characteristic of the former are the pretentious verbs *involucrar* and *inmiscuirse* and Latinisms like *ad hoc* and *sui generis*, whereas the latter suffered from the illusion that *eppur si muove* (Galileo's famous, though legendary, aside − 'and yet it moves') meant *por si acaso*.

Devices of this type are essentially signposts, very necessary to guide the reader through such extensive territory. A deeper level of characterization needs, as we shall see, subtler means. The use of eccentricities and *muletillas* tends, especially if employed as the only element of characterization, to produce 'flat' characters type-cast for the rôle assigned to them, but at the same time they provide some of the best opportunities for humour. It is among the 'flat' characters, too, that the figures repeated from one novel to another are usually drawn. Figures like José Ido −the recurring character *par exellence*− Federico Ruiz and Villalonga have a similar functional rôle in several novels.

The rôle of minor characters is predominantly functional, to link characters or social strata or to throw light on the major characters. In *Fortunata*, however, there is a marked tendency, as Montesinos has pointed out, for characters to develop full-blooded personalities of their own: 'es increíble hasta qué punto puede llegar la autonomía de estas figuras' (*16*, II, p. 216). He singles out Mauricia *la dura* as an acceptable expansion of her functional rôle, but finds Juan Pablo and Nicolás Rubín, and especially Don Basilio Andrés de la Caña, superfluous. Certainly Galdós allows himself an extremely wide scope and lets some of his incidents develop almost independently of the main action, as few examples chosen at random will demonstrate. The meeting of Ido and Izquierdo (I, ix, 4), when Ido eats meat with such devastating consequences and Izquierdo launches forth on his political denunciations, is one such incident; though Ido's illusions about his wife's fidelity and Izquierdo's revolutionary stance have their importance in the structure of the novel, this and similar episodes are undeniably elaborated in an unhurried fashion and *con amore*. The same may be said of the leisured development of the important episode of Mauricia's disturbances in Las Micaelas (II, vi, 8-10) after she had stolen Sor Marcela's bottle of brandy, or of the café gossip of Juan Pablo, Relimpio, La Caña and the *Pater* (III, i,

3-6); in this latter case, in particular, Montesinos's strictures seem justified.

Associated with minor characters and their sometimes inflated development is an extraordinary richness of anecdote on which much of the humour of the novel depends. A few examples will suffice. The one shameful incident in Estupiñá's life was when he got drunk and took a nightwatchman's lantern for the Viaticum (I, iii, 2); and during his illness the unliterary Plácido fell avidly upon the *Boletín Eclesiástico de la Diócesis de Lugo* as the only reading matter available (I, iii, 4). When Juan Pablo is expounding his newly acquired philosophy of Nature, one of the street-traders, recalling her confessor's reference to *esas naturalezas*, thought he was referring to her well-developed bosom (III, i, 6, p. 308).

The household of Doña Lupe is particularly rich in these anecdotes. For example, when Doña Lupe herself ignores Nicolás's repeated requests for strawberries but brings home secretly a punnet and divides it between herself and Maxi, leaving a few also for Papitos (II, iv, 6); or when she instructs Papitos as to how she is to prepare for the greedy cleric the hake which had gone bad by smothering it with salt and coating it with flour (II, v, 2); or when the indignant Papitos hangs out Doña Lupe's false breast in full view on the washing line on the balcony, only to think better of it before her mistress returned (II, v, 2). Into the same category come Olimpia's incessant practising of the piano piece she never quite managed to finish correctly (IV, i, 4) and the trick Segismundo Ballester planned of administering a laxative (which he pretended was poison) disguised as a sweet for his enemy the critic Ponce (IV, i, 9).

At times Galdós seems aware of the danger of letting his characters get out of hand. It is noteworthy that he drastically pruned the rôle of Doña Barbarita which was far more prominent in the manuscript version. It was she, not Jacinta, who originally disliked Villalonga as having an undesirable influence on Juanito. Similarly, Juan Pablo Rubín had a different and more extended rôle. He was originally 20 years older than Maxi and lavished a paternal affection on him.

We have seen that four figures —Doña Lupe, Doña Guillermina, Mauricia *la dura* and Feijoo— have an importance second only to that of the four principals and that they are all concerned in the development of Fortunata. Of these Doña Lupe is the most individualized person, who intervenes constantly but always according to the previously established norms of her character: she lacks any creative development of her own or any inner tension. At the same time, she is the richest comic creation both in her own actions and, as we have seen, in the environment which she dominates. The startlingly ugly portrait of her late husband Jáuregui, with eyes which like Kitchener in the recruiting posters follow the spectator, and the strident colouring of the metallic accoutrements, surrounded most unsymmetrically by a large number of photographs, is a fine example of her dubious taste.

Doña Lupe's basic characteristic is indicated by the physical disability already referred to: her artificial breast, insensible to compassion, represents her ruthless money-lending activities. Her mercenary instincts take many amusing or ironical forms: she pardons Mauricia's debt to her of a paltry 53 *reales*, expressing the wish that it had been all of 200 *reales* (III, vi, 1, p. 370). She is prejudiced in Fortunata's favour by her thrifty impulses and later resolves to promote a reconciliation with Maxi when Fortunata entrusts 2,000 *duros* to her to invest without asking for a receipt: money for her is in itself a *prima facie* sign of respectability. Moreover, to ensure the reconciliation she has no compunction in falsifying Fortunata's economic situation to Maxi by speaking of deprivations and shortage of food. Treating her beauty in commercial terms, she is disgusted by Fortunata's failure to exploit her relationship with Juanito: 'Pues si efectivamente no le ha dado nada', she declares, 'hay que reconocer que ese hombre es el mayor de los indecentes' (IV, i, 6, p. 430). As for Fortunata: 'Por no saber, no sabes siquiera perderte' (IV, i, 9, p. 436). Similarly she encourages Maxi to invent a panacea: 'una cosa que lo cure todo, absolutamente todo, y que se pueda vender en líquido, en píldoras, pastillas, cápsulas, jarabe, emplasto y en cigarros aspiradores' (IV, i, 1, p. 416). Even the most insignificant things count; Doña Lupe instructs Papitos to use the next-door shoe-scraper, to save their own (III, v, 3, p. 363).

Doña Lupe has, however, other qualities as well as money-grabbing. She is methodical and efficient, a 'reloj con alma' (III, v, 1, p. 356), who delights above all in directing people, whether it is her three nephews, Papitos or Fortunata: hence her acquiescence in Maxi's marriage and in Fortunata's return. When she rightly suspects that Fortunata has become Juanito's lover again, it is the loss of power, personal as well as financial, over her that she regrets. And she has strong social ambitions, centred on Doña Guillermina, without sharing in any way her sense of self-sacrifice, as she watches the *santa y fundadora*'s movement to and from her orphanage. Her story of Feijoo's courtship of her, true or false, is also an aspect of her pretensions. On this account she attends the communion for Mauricia at her sickbed, but is disappointed that 'por lo que yo voy viendo, aquí no viene más *dama* que yo' (III, vi, 3, p. 375). To gain a reputation for charity at no cost, she offers to pass a night of vigil with her, but is careful not to be too easily available for money contributions.

Don Evaristo González Feijoo is much more limited in scope since his rôle is essentially that of influencing Fortunata. He is first introduced, however, as a member of Juan Pablo Rubín's *tertulia*, and shown as indulgent with the passions and enthusiasms of others which he claims to have outgrown. He is profoundly sceptical about politics, which he believes to be a farce, and the only important question concerns individuals: who is to be supported and who is not (III, i, 1). It is an attitude which is typical of the climate of the Restoration, which Don Evaristo applies by recommending Juan Pablo, Nicolás and Villaamil (without success in the last case) to his influential friend Villalonga. His attitude to private life is equally relativistic: fickleness is the law of the universe. It is for this reason that despite many affairs he has never married. Social conventions should be adhered to or at least not openly flouted: forms, not principles, are essential. At the same time it is dangerous to be carried away by one's heart; one should endeavour to keep oneself in check —*no descomponerse*. Yet his own last fling, with Fortunata, which brings him a momentary rejuvenescence, must be held responsible for his alarmingly rapid physical decline. His protection of Fortunata is conducted with the utmost prudence and he arranges the 'restoration' with admirable discretion, squashing forthrightly Juan Pablo's suspicions with all the concealed authority wielded by a creditor owed money; securing a canonry for Nicolás; giving money to Fortunata for Doña Lupe to invest, together with admirable advice on how to handle the lady. Above all, he presents to Fortunata an alternative line of conduct, of dissembling and keeping up appearances.

Critics have found it difficult to determine where Galdós stands on this issue. Kindly, tolerant and detached, Feijoo is often taken as a portrait of Galdós himself (*17*, p. 85; *16*, II, p. 266). In my view this is a misleading idea, largely conceived by hindsight, since Galdós was about 43 when he created his practical philosopher of 69. He may have had a certain sympathy for his ideas on love and marriage, on preserving the forms of conduct and even on a political system of tolerance and personal patronage; he appears to be saying that this is how life works; but there is little doubt too that he admired also the passion and sincerity —in the last resort irrepressible— represented by Fortunata. In any case it is important to remember that Galdós is presenting not models of conduct, but interacting attitudes such as constitute a sample of those which prevail in life. Feijoo offers one practical solution to the problems of living in society, but it is not the only one presented and for Fortunata it is ultimately not successful.

Mauricia *la dura* and Doña Guillermina are the most interesting of the developed characters. Unlike Feijoo or Doña Lupe, they have spiritual problems or aspirations which brook of no easy solution. They are clearly juxtaposed the one to the other, as Gustavo Correa (*11*, pp. 110-15) and Ricardo Gullón (*31*, pp. 159-67) have indicated, and appear to constitute a clearcut opposition of Good and Evil impinging on Fortunata: 'la polaridad de lo demoníaco y lo angélico, encarnada en dos personajes antagónicos . . .' (*31*, p. 159). The reiterated identification of Mauricia with *lo satánico* and Guillermina and Jacinta with saintly or angelic qualities would seem to justify this, but the question in my view is not a simple as it appears.

Let us take Mauricia first. She is given a full study such as befits a major character, but this does not justify considering her outside the context of the novel, or finding her Dostoyevskian or Nietzschean. The reasons for her full development lie essentially within the novel, and are intimately connected with Fortunata; discussion of much of her activities and her personality will therefore be postponed for the moment. What we can discuss now are her general characteristics. The sustained comparison with Napoleon gives her a romantic and revolutionary cast, but her voice and coarse language destroy this illusion (II, vi, 1): her rebellion is instinctive, individual, brutal and uncontrolled, 'satanic' to those around her. Galdós gives us a fairly detailed clinical description of the various stages of her periodical outbursts (II, vi, 2), but this does not fully explain what causes them. They do not appear to derive directly from her alcoholism, which in any case may be a symptom rather than a cause. Sor Natividad attributes these disorders to 'males de nervios', clearly an insufficient explanation but one which at least implies psychological disturbance. The treatment she receives is obviously inadequate, but it may be noted that she responds to a sympathetic approach by Sor Marcela, although her violence always breaks out again.

The episode which reveals most about her is the long and violent incident in Las Micaelas after she claims to have seen the Virgin. The cognac stolen from Sor Marcela provides an obvious but not complete explanation for her behaviour; her urge to steal the Monstrance demonstrates, together with much unassimilated superstition, an inner spiritual impulse which remains unsatisfied and which Galdós's narrator does not seek to elucidate: 'Por grande que sea un absurdo, siempre tiene cabida en el inconmensurable hueco de la mente humana' (II, vi, 9, p. 256; *19*, pp. 424-6). She gets, incidentally, precious little help from society, at least until she is dying. Her truculent defiance of everyone in this incident, including Doña Guillermina and Fortunata, is met with like treatment: she is struck by the priest Don León Pintado and, at Guillermina's suggestion, thrown out of Las Micaelas; Fortunata, who might have calmed her down, is kept away from her (*19*, pp. 279-81). So much for real concern with the redemption of sinners!

More than a personification of Evil, Mauricia reveals in her own self the struggle between an impulse towards uncontrolled rebellion and remorse for this lack of discipline. This is particularly apparent in the important death-bed scenes which exercise such an influence on Fortunata.

Doña Guillermina also has her share of ambivalence. As Leslie Brooks (*44*) has pointed out, her charitable causes, though undertaken with complete dedication, are established ones within the norms of the rich bourgeois society from which she springs. Ricardo Gullón (*31*, p. 162) calls her 'la santa burguesa'. About the installation of

Don Alfonso XII, she can say with complete conviction: 'le hemos traído con esa condición: que favorezca la beneficencia y la religión' (III, ii, 1, p. 310). Her religious ideas are orthodox and unbending: she picturesquely affirms Spanish spiritual superiority: ' ¡Qué importará que haya pulgas con tal que haya cristiandad!' (III, ii, 4, p. 320); she confines girls like Felisa in Las Micaelas on no authority but her own (II, vi, 6, p. 245); she stoutly refuses to accept the benevolent actions of the Protestants Don Horacio and Doña Malvina on Mauricia's behalf and is willing to flout the law in doing so; the Civil Guard will obey her instructions without question. Of the two institutions with which she is associated, Las Micaelas, certainly, has few redeeming features, and we may suspect that the orphanage, to which *el Pitusin* is consigned, will be equally grim. It is striking that when Guillermina's vocation as *virgen y fundadora* is described at length (I, vii, 1), all the emphasis is laid on her powers of initiative and her capacity for command and organization. No indication at all is given of compassion. In fact, in her dealings with the poor, she is authoritarian, severely practical and more than somewhat patronizing: 'Porque se encuentran almas buenas, sí —decía—; pero también mucha ingratitud . . . la propia miseria les ataca el corazón a muchos y se lo corrompe. A mí me han insultado . . .' (I, vii, 2, p. 80). The charity distributed to the poor of the 'Cuarto Estado' merely scratches the surface and Doña Guillermina seems to have no conception of any deeper or more permanent solutions. Her criticism of the taverns as the source of crime in the slums ('De aquí salen todos los crímenes', I, ix, 1, p. 99) is a particularly shallow and complacent one. As Brooks (*44*, pp. 87-8) has shown, the contrast with Benina in *Misericordia* shows what true compassion and charity really are. On personal moral issues, too, her standards inevitably reflect her class: her severity with Fortunata is not matched by any comparable severity with Juanito.

It is true that Galdós appears to praise unconditionally, at the very time of writing the novel, the lady Doña Ernestina Manuel de Villena, on whom Doña Guillermina is modelled (*43*). In my view, this illustrates once more the crucial difference between a biography and a character in fiction. No doubt Galdós sincerely admired disinterested charitable work and projected Doña Ernestina's worthy dedication onto Guillermina, but for the purposes of his story he needed to integrate his character within the fictitious world he was creating. Guillermina represents as a consequence a model of conventional sanctity within a society which she does not question in any way. Indeed in this absolute devotion to her religion, her indefatigable energy and her eagerness to undertake the most distasteful of tasks there seems to be a certain measure of frustration: longing for a sacrifice which she has never had to make because she has freely chosen her mode of life, she urges sacrifice on others (Fortunata, her nephew Manuel Moreno-Isla). In a Galdosian world of uncertainties and ambiguities[23] she has blind confidence in accepting and even interpreting what she takes to be God's will. Although she has moments of self-reproach, on lying to Fortunata (III, vii, 3), and of doubt, about the rightness of Fortunata's assault on Aurora (IV, vi, 10, p. 529; IV, vi, 11, p. 532), her immutable principles are bound to the prevailing social order, in which moreover most standards are relative, as a comparison with Doña Lupe and Feijoo, in their different ways, will show. We shall see how Doña Guillermina's absolute faith in a static divinely-ordered world, sympathetically expounded throughout the novel, is finally called into question at the end. The simple equation of Doña Guillermina with Good, as of Mauricia with Evil, is insufficient to capture the complexity of Galdós's view of life.

---

[23]It is worth recalling here Galdós's remarks in reply to Pereda's inaugural address to the Academy in 1897: 'Pereda no duda; yo sí. Siempre he visto mis convicciones obscurecidas en alguna parte por sombras que venían de no sé dónde. El es un espíritu sereno, yo un espíritu turbado, inquieto . . .' (*Discursos*, p. 154).

VI The principal characters

The two main characters who are introduced first —the Santa Cruz couple— are less highly developed than Maxi and Fortunata. This is not a question of a failure in characterization; it corresponds, rather, to the remarkable degree of individual development in both Maxi and Fortunata compared with their more conventional counterparts.

First, Juanito Santa Cruz. We have already seen how he is handled from the point of view of the narrator and how closely he fits into a social and political pattern. It now remains to consider the individual character traits with which Galdós has endowed him. In the early description of him at the age of 24 (I, i, 1, pp. 14-15), Galdós's narrator, by a series of oblique contrasts and qualifications, stresses the essential superficiality of the man. He is 'muy simpático', but his appearance is superior to the way he deals with people; he impresses by his fluency without really putting himself out; his knowledge seems greater than it is; he excels in slick paradoxes; he talks too much. Finally, by the comparison, deftly modified in Juanito's favour, with the despicable Joaquín Pez, the seducer of Isidora in *La desheredada*, he is represented as not quite 'un verdadero botarate'. The characteristic and inevitable diminutive applied to him is partly explained in a way which makes it sound like a feature of the national virtue of 'familiaridad democrática' combining courtesy and confident behaviour. In fact, the diminutive has mostly unfavourable implications. It indicates the apron-strings to which he is tied ('ternuras domésticas'), and his favoured position ('hábitos de servidumbre'). Insofar as he is a Don Juan, he is an inferior specimen. It also suggests frivolity, wit, urbanity and by implication superficiality, some of the qualities associated with Galdós's fellow-novelist Juan Valera, who is mentioned as one destined to be known by a diminutive most of his life. More important, it brands him, without saying so directly, as a *señorito*: an idle and well-off young man about town. Our narrator goes on to put the best possible gloss on Juanito's dabbling in study quickly followed by total abandonment of scholarly pursuits:

Ni extrañará nadie que un chico guapo, poseedor del arte de

agradar y del arte de vestir, hijo único de padres ricos, inteligente,
instruido, de frase seductora en la conversación, pronto en las
respuestas, agudo y ocurrente en los juicios, un chico, en fin, al
cual se le podría poner el rótulo social de *brillante*, considerara
ocioso y hasta ridículo el meterse a averiguar si hubo o no un
idioma único primitivo, etc. (I, i, 1, p. 15)

Juanito thus makes a distinction between life experienced at first
hand and reading about it, but his way of living is both contrived
and inconstant; the word applied most frequently to his scheming
being *triquiñuelas*: 'dodges'. Moreover, the example used to illustrate
the difference —eating a chop and hearing a description of the
digestive process— neatly anticipates the heartless caprice with which
he enjoys witnessing José Ido's ravenous consumption of chops and
its disastrous consequences.

We have seen that the narrator employs at this stage a technique of
underplaying the moral implications of Juanito's conduct. Similarly,
his complete lack of occupation is emphasized, not explicitly as it is
later (I, viii, 2, p. 85: 'Por lo dicho se habrá comprendido que el
Delfín era un hombre enteramente despreocupado'), but in the
account of how, to the great consternation of his mother, he comes
to make his first trip to Paris (I, i, 2, pp. 16-18). The casually
dropped details of the business which motivated the journey of his
companions Villalonga and Federico Ruiz throw into relief the fact
that Juanito is even more idle than his fellows.

From the incidental comments on the cossetted and pampered
upbringing of this long-awaited only son it emerges clearly that he
has not acquired the responsibility of a mature human being. Assisted
in his lessons at school, sheltered from the consequences of his
intervention in the *Noche de San Daniel* by the impeccable respectability of his father, watched over anxiously by a possessive mother
in his early youth, he has his wife despotically chosen for him and
the circumstances of the holiday at Plencia contrived to foster the
engagement. Doña Bárbara considers the marriage as a sort of
prolongation of, and substitute for, her maternal care. Moreover,
Juanito is constantly referred to in childish terms: 'niño bonito',
'niño mimado', 'nene', etc., and the infantile language the young
couple use on their honeymoon is not without significance; on more
than one occasion, both on the honeymoon and later when he is ill,
Juanito is evidently mothered also by his wife. And of course the

young couple live in the same house where they can remain under the thumb of the parents.

The one moment of self-revelation in Juanito's life occurs when he gets drunk in Seville (I, v, 5-7). Then, without losing his pedantry, he reveals the strong attraction Fortunata and the world of the *pueblo* exercised over him and at the same time his awareness —prudently concealed or played down at other times— of his shameful responsibility for Fortunata's fate compared with her blind confidence in him. 'Esa sinceridad brutal y disparatada que sólo puede compararse al vómito físico, producido por un emético muy fuerte' (p. 64) is in marked contrast with his normal sophisticated arguments, 'la maquinaria, más brillante que sólida, de su raciocinio' (p. 63), 'sus triquiñuelas de hombre leído y mundano' (p. 64), when 'sus declaraciones eran una verdad refundida como las comedias antiguas. El amor propio no le permitía la reproducción fiel de los hechos' (p. 62).

The narrator has now become more categorical and less elusive about a figure he has until now skilfully built up by dint of contrast and insinuation. He comments directly on the alternations of pleasures he sought:

> Juan tenía temporadas. En épocas periódicas y casi fijas se hastiaba de sus correrías, y entonces su mujer, tan mona y cariñosa, le ilusionaba *como si fuera la mujer de otro.* (I, vii, 1, p. 84)

The italicized phrase, repeated on other occasions, is worth noticing: no sense of loyalty or duty or remorse is involved in his periodical return to his wife: she represents after a time simply another innovation: 'así lo muy antiguo y conocido se convierte en nuevo', with a hankering after *lo prohibido* —another man's wife— about it. 'No era aquello virtud' —we are told later— 'sino cansancio del pecado; no era el sentimiento puro y regular del orden, sino el hastío de la revolución' (III, ii, 2, p. 311). The fact that he loves his wife only makes things worse, stressing his selfishness and irresponsibility. To his depraved epicurean taste purity itself has its savour once in a while:

> Vicioso y discreto, sibarita y hombre de talento, aspirando a la erudición de todos los goces y con bastante buen gusto para espiritualizar las cosas materiales, no podía contentarse con gustar la belleza comprada o conquistada, la gracia, el donaire, la extravagancia; quería gustar también la virtud, no precisamente

la vencida, que deja de serlo, sino la pura, que en su pureza misma tenía para él su picante. (I, viii, 1, p. 85)

Other traits also emerge. His extraordinary vanity is constantly in evidence, but his environment continues to have its share of the blame, for his high opinion of himself is shared by those around him. He is mean, and his studied carefulness about money undoubtedly corresponds to his meanness of spirit. This young man, in contrast with the many *señoritos* who fall victim to Torquemada, is too calculating to contract debts or *hacer locuras*.

At the end of Book I, Juanito experiences his one moment of strong emotion in his frantic search for Fortunata which results in his attack of pneumonia. At the root of this passion, apparently out of character, lies his insatiable search for novelty —the new elegant Fortunata described by Villalonga, now fallen on bad times again—combined with pique at not getting his own way. On tracking her down eventually at the very moment of her wedding, he has no compunction whatever about his action, and his cynical comment that 'Ya sé que te has casado. Has hecho bien' (II, vii, 6, p. 277) shocks Fortunata. When he breaks with her, at Jacinta's instigation but with relief, that narrator gives us the most categorical statement about his actions. The moment is appropriate, since this is the last time we shall see Juanito at the front of the stage. His rôle is henceforth passive; in the fleeting glimpse we have of their next and final liaison Fortunata has a sense of purpose of her own, and he has no part in determining the eventual outcome of the novel. Galdós wishes to emphasise finally with an authorial voice the dimensions of the perfidy to which his scorn for what he possessed and his yearning for what he did not have led him. The despicable nature of his second affair with Fortunata is brought out:

Cuando ella salió del convento con corona de honrada para casarse; cuando llevaba mezcladas en su pecho las azucenas de la purificación religiosa y los azahares de la boda, parecíale al *Delfín* digna y lucida hazaña arrancarla de aquella vida. (III, iii, 1, p. 321)

It is further reiterated in the phrase which follows: 'aquella situación revolucionaria que había implantado pisoteando los derechos de dos matrimonios', and which recalls Nicolás Rubín's unjust censure of Fortunata: 'Váyase usted a correr aventuras, deshonre a su marido, perturbe dos matrimonios' (II, vii, 12, p. 292). As Fortunata bitterly complains when next abandoned: 'Después que hemos cometido todos los crímenes ahora salimos con escrúpulos . . . Y yo pago la falta de los dos' (III, iii, 1, p. 323).

In the rupture he picks on anything he can to ease his situation: Feijoo's visit; her lack of ostentation in not wearing the silk dressing-gown he had bought her; her popular taste in food. He lies about his parents' knowledge of the affair; he speaks of principles; and he advises her to return to the husband from whom he has so callously snatched her. We are left in no doubt about where the responsibility for the events of the novel lie: in the perfidious, vain, superficial and utterly selfish personality of Juanito Santa Cruz. Juanito's personality is too shallow to give much scope for subtlety or surprise, and he is accordingly presented in a somewhat external and explicit fashion. Within these limits however the portrayal is a successful one.

Jacinta is often dismissed as a character of little interest, dominated to the exclusion of all else by her obsession with children, but there are deeper aspects to her portrayal. First, there is the contrast between the apparent and the real situation she finds herself in. Viewed from outside she makes a brilliant match, having been chosen especially in unpromising circumstances by her aunt to be her daughter-in-law. Her inner state of mind is however very different. Jacinta is described in terms which suggest an affectionate, gentle, rather than passionate, nature; her nickname 'Mona del cielo' and the repeated image of 'paloma' reflect this. Pretty rather than beautiful, she has a certain fragility implicit in her name ('hyacinth'), and seems destined to age early: 'Por su talle delicado y su figura y cara porcelanescas, revelaba ser una de esas hermosuras a quienes la Naturaleza concede poco tiempo de esplendor, y que se ajan pronto, en cuanto les toca la primera pena de la vida o la maternidad' (I, iv, 2, p. 46). It is of course sorrow rather than motherhood which will wither her. She is subsequently described –by Moreno-Isla– as having locks of premature grey hair (IV, ii, 3, p. 451), but his devotion is a testimony to her attractions. These qualities do not exclude a gradual increase in independent spirit, foreshadowed by the 'ciertas tenacidades de carácter' Barbarita noted in her. Like most girls of her class, she is portrayed as ignorant of all but a few social graces, but she does learn from experience to adopt opinions of her own. Her first moments of awareness come during her honeymoon. Galdós delicately hints at the innocent girl's hesitant initiation

into the joys of married life (her mother-in-law's early days of marriage are described in similar terms), but in the confession she gradually
winkles out of her husband she is soon disagreeably struck by the
term of endearment *nena* which she has inherited. When she meditates
on the wretchedness of the girls who work in a Barcelona factory,
she draws a conclusion which is surprisingly relevant and acute: 'se
vuelven tan tontas, digo, que en cuanto se les presenta un pillo
cualquiera se dejan seducir . . . Y no es maldad; es que llega un
momento en que dicen: 'Vale más ser mujer mala que máquina
buena' (I, v, 3, p. 54). Juanito's drunken revelations that Fortunata
adored him and that he treated her despicably with the contempt of
the rich for the poor are followed later by an exclamation of sympathy by Jacinta '– ¡Pobres mujeres! –exclamó–. Siempre la peor
parte para ellas' (I, v, 7, p. 63). In contrast with Juanito's 'dialéctica
convencional con la cual se prueba todo lo que se quiere', she
experiences, not just pride at having won him, but also 'una protesta
contra el ultraje y despiadado abandono de la desconocida'.

Jacinta's increasing frustration at having no children deserves
more sympathy than it gets from the complacent, closed family
circle round her. It makes her bitterly envious of poor women with
children in a way which parallels Fortunata's discontent with her
marriage. It causes her to be rebellious against her fate, against God
even, for denying her children while giving them in such excess to
her mother and her sisters. The frustration comes to a head in two
significant incidents. The first occurs, after a quarrel with her sister
Candelaria over spoiling her children, when Jacinta strives to save
some kittens from drowning in the drains (I, vi, 4); it is a moving
episode in which she first thinks the mewing is a baby's cry, then
gets the porter, Deogracias, to try and rescue the kittens and even
contemplates having the paving stones removed to do so. The second
(I, viii, 2) consists of the vivid and convincing dream she had at a
performance at the Teatro Real in which a man-child tried to unbut-
ton her dress and feed himself at her breast. Her obsession is also
poignantly captured in the 'visita al Cuarto Estado' (I, ix, 1) when
the external reality becomes an 'imagen borrosa' as her mind concen-
trates more and more on the children –alive or dead– and the
'tantísima madre por aquellos barrios'.

Jacinta's troubles, baseless to her family circle, but very real to her, do not stop here. Though it is less important to her than her yearning for children, she also has her justified suspicions about her husband's faithfulness which she cannot reveal and which she initially resolves to bear patiently. Then Ido's visit —which in contrast with Juanito she found distressing— gives rise to the crucial episode of *el Pitusín* which might have produced a partial solution to her frustration but which in fact only added to it. Among other things, the visits to the 'Cuarto Estado' make her aware of the grinding poverty of the slums, and cause her to scatter gifts somewhat indiscriminately around her and to protect Mauricia's daughter, Adoración. Her immediate and overpowering attachment to the supposed son of Juanito and Fortunata corresponds more to her imperative desire to satisfy her longing for a child than to objective realities. She does not foresee the inevitable objections of the Santa Cruz family; and she sees in him an imaginary likeness to Juanito, while dreading some resemblance to the hated Fortunata. The subject of false coins discussed at the shopkeeper Villuendas' house just as Juanín is brought to them raises the question of his genuineness which she does not face. The family view her as an 'inocentona' and, significantly enough, the climax when Juanito confronts Juanín occurs on the *día de Inocentes* (28 December), the Spanish equivalent of April Fool's Day: Jacinta's action is treated as the biggest *inocentada* of all. The complete dominance, no less real for being veiled and benevolent, of the elder Santa Cruz couple is now openly exercised. Jacinta has been since her marriage utterly subservient in the administration of the joint household to her mother-in-law —'despotismo ilustrado' it is called on one occasion— and entirely dependent on her and, through her, on Don Baldomero, for money. The *Pitusín* affair produces a complete closing of the ranks against Jacinta's project; Barbarita's reluctant acquiescence gives way rapidly before Don Baldomero's disapproval, and Jacinta's aims, first of adopting the boy herself and then of having her sister bring him up, are firmly rejected: Juanín goes to Doña Guillermina's orphanage, against Jacinta's earlier vehement refusal. 'Quien manda manda', and Jacinta can do no more about it than Fortunata can against the powerful forces in society which inevitably prevail against her.

Some time later, just as the Restoration is taking place (January

1875), when faced with evidence of Juanito's renewed liaison with Fortunata, she feels like breaking out of the family straitjacket. Her indignation encompasses all those rejoicing around her and extends to the new King, associated with her sorrows. It is the familiar rebellious attitude deriving from frustration.

The later stages of the development of Jacinta's personality depend on her direct relationship with Fortunata, which will be dealt with later. We shall see how the implications of the traits just discussed come to fulfilment in the conclusion of the novel.

Although she is undoubtedly the most important character in the novel, Fortunata comes into prominence remarkably late. In the first two parts, after the fleeting scene in which she meets Juanito, she is viewed indirectly, through the eyes of other characters (Juanito, Villalonga, Maxi); there is no narrative account of her circumstances as occurs with all the other principal characters. Similarly, no detailed description from outside is given, but a physical portrait is gradually built up through the impressions of the characters. Juanito speaks of her 'ojos como estrellas'; Villalonga praises 'aquel cuerpo sin igual', 'aquel busto estatuario'; Maxi finds her 'la más extraordinaria hermosura que hasta entonces habían visto sus ojos'; she herself is rather ingenuously pleased with her good looks as she looks at herself in the mirror and comments, among other features, on her 'ojos negros tan bonitos que . . . *le daban la puñalada al Espiritui Santo*', her milk-white teeth and her abundant black hair; Papitos contrasts maliciously and enviously her well-proportioned figure with Doña Lupe's false bust. Her robust health and animal vitality are constantly brought out.

The essential personal quality which gradually emerges is her straightforward sincerity —in Galdós's words 'Lo mejorcito que aquella mujer tenía era su ingenuidad' (II, ii, 1, p. 174). It is an aspect of her simple unintellectual approach to life: 'lo que sale de *entre mí*'. It is quite in accord with Galdós's subtle sense of the paradoxes of existence that a girl who has sunk to prostitution and suffered the most degrading experiences should serve in a certain way and without false sentiment as an example of faithfulness and honesty. As Feijoo testifies: 'Y lo más raro es que después de tanto manosear hayan quedado intactas ciertas prendas, como la sinceridad, que, al fin, es algo, y la constancia en el amor a uno solo'

(III, iv, 4, p. 336). Ballester emotionally rams home the paradox after her death, declaring to the astonished Guillermina that she was 'la persona más honrada y honesta que usted puede imaginar' (IV, vi, 15, p. 541).

The slow emergence of her personality is of fundamental importance. Sherman Eoff gives a detailed account of her psychological makeup and her 'adjustive behaviour' (*13*, pp. 46-9). At the outset she appears to be completely passive, a figure who is worked upon but who hardly acts for herself. Thanks to Juanito her life has taken a course over which she has very little control. In her shame and despair she has indulged in her degradation to spite society and spite herself, but has conceived a loathing for her life as a woman of the streets. When Maxi encounters her she is listless and easily led. Her self-esteem, in Eoff's terminology (*24*, p. 271), is at its lowest ebb. She has therefore everything to gain by agreeing to marry him, though all her instincts are against it. Her contradictory feelings emerge on one night in particular (II, ii, 8), which she later discovers was while Juanito was suffering from pneumonia. After wondering whether Juanito remembers her, she determines to accept Maxi. With great satisfaction she prepares his favourite meal for him, but once it is ready is assaulted once more by physical repugnance. She then makes a revealing comparison with a weathervane:

> Ella misma comparó su alma en aquellos días a una veleta. Tan pronto marcaba para un lado como para otro. De improviso, como si se levantara un fuerte viento, la veleta daba la vuelta grande y ponía la punta donde antes tenía la cola. (pp. 188-9)

Later, she thinks of herself as having been taken off to be married as animals are taken to the slaughterhouse. Similarly, she confides to Juanito:

> Me dejé meter en las Micaelas y me dejé casar. . . . ¿Sabes tú cómo fue todo eso? Pues como lo que cuentan de que *manetizan* a una persona y hacen de ella lo que quieren: lo mismito. Yo, cuando no se trata de querer, no tengo voluntad. Me traen y me llevan como una muñeca. (II, vii, 7, p. 279)

It is the same feeling which she afterwards voices to Doña Guillermina: 'me casé sin saber lo que hacía' (III, vi, 10, p. 397). The combined efforts of Maxi himself, and of Doña Lupe and Nicolás, for reasons of their own, together with the superficial and superstitious religious sentiments instilled in her in Las Micaelas, persuade her to marry

Maxi. Inevitably her motives are misinterpreted: she did not seek to gain freedom to do as she liked, as Mauricia advised and Doña Guillermina suspected, but made a genuine though —given Juanito's predatory instincts and Maxi's inadequacy— hopeless effort to achieve an honourable position.

But there is no hesitation where her love for Juanito is concerned. On falling into the carefully prepared trap Juanito has set for her directly after her marriage, she acts automatically without premeditation or any regard for outside considerations: 'Se consideraba Fortunata en aquel caso como ciego mecanismo que recibe impulso de sobrenatural mano' (II, vii, 6, p. 277). All the notions of conventional conduct inculcated in her by Maxi and the nuns fall off her; she is as if intoxicated. Yet this irresistible instinct corresponds to an extremely acute, though not clearly formulated, sense of 'natural law', which signifies that the man who seduced her under promise of marriage and whose child she bore is her true husband: a proposition which the narrator calls a 'satánica convicción' when she declares to Juanito 'mi marido eres tú ... ; todo lo demás ... ¡papas!' (p. 278). This is followed shortly after by the idea that *'querer a quien se quiere no puede ser cosa mala'* (p. 279). The conviction is 'satanic' (the word links her with Mauricia) only in that it flouts the institutions on which society is based. She is frequently said —by Doña Guillermina, by Maxi, by Juanito, as well as by the narrator himself— to lack all moral sense, but this must be treated with caution; what she lacks is any regard for legal forms or social conventions, which are equated in a deliberately facile way with morality. When Juanito subsequently deserts her, Fortunata's notion is put more clearly: 'Lo que Fortunata había pensado era que el amor salva todas las irregularidades, mejor dicho, que el amor lo hace todo regular, que rectifica las leyes, derogando las que se le oponen' (III, iii, 1, p. 323). Her sincerity is appalled at the ease with which Juanito evokes principles whose consequences she alone has to bear and the cynicism of his advice to return to her husband.

This is not to say that her urge towards respectability is not sincere or that she is not conscious of the enormity of her personal betrayal of Maxi. Later, the strength of her desire for honourable status (see Eoff, *23*, pp. 131-8; *24*, pp. 271-5) is forcibly brought out, but she remains inevitably the plaything of others. Her resistance to accepting the protection of Feijoo is genuine though useless, simply because there was no possible outlet —as Galdós was never tired of pointing out (think of the case of Amparo in *Tormento*)— for an uneducated girl in the Madrid of the late nineteenth century except to sell her sexual favours. Feijoo's solution was the least dishonourable course open to her. Moreover, Fortunata's lack of guile made her quite unsuitable as a courtesan. It is worth noticing the telling detail that she does not like camelias and that one of the few books she knew was the story of the renowned courtesan, the younger Dumas's *La Dame aux camélias*, the original of *La Traviata*. She continues to be torn between remorse and a sense of guiltlessness: 'su conciencia giraba sobre un pivote, presentándole ya el lado blanco ya el lado negro' (III, iv, 3, p. 333). At one moment she indulges in self-recrimination: 'la mujer más mala que ha nacido', 'lo *desaborida* que soy', 'ordinariota y salvaje', at others she fixes on Jacinta, who becomes increasingly the target of her revenge and the object of her envy. In the agony of being abandoned, her first intention was to enter the Santa Cruz house and attack Jacinta. Then she proceeds to pour scorn on her rival's honour ('a mí no me digan que es virtuosa', p. 325) before she settles down to assert her own: 'soy honrada'. Later, she speaks to Feijoo about her ambivalent attitude to Jacinta and he reproves her for her doubts about Jacinta's virtue; but she also admits her envious admiration for Juanito's legal wife.

Apart from the salutary physical effect of their short affair, for her beauty blossoms as never before, Feijoo's influence provides a possible escape. His 'filosofía práctica' offers her the chance of curbing the spontaneous sincerity which characterizes her and of introducing moderation and if necessary duplicity instead of violent passions ('rasgos': see Gilman, *18*, pp. 313-14) into her actions. In the 'restoration' which he succeeds in effecting, Fortunata has greater scope than before for controlling her own life. But she is exposed also to other influences, notably Mauricia *la dura* and Doña Guillermina, and her rivalry with Jacinta has yet to reach its culmination. These crucial factors will be examined in a separate section.

The creation of Maximiliano Rubín is generally recognized as a major achievement. Far from being a static character, he is the figure who shows the most varied and original development in the course of the novel. His high-sounding Imperial name shows Galdós's irony at its cruellest.

The initial impression he produces could hardly be more unpromising. His growth is stunted, his physical strength negligible; he suffers from constant migraines, nasal congestion and spots. He is extremely ugly, with very thin hair inclining to premature baldness, exceedingly irregular teeth and an abnormally flattened nose. As the novel develops, the living beings with which he is consistently compared are insects or crustaceans. At the beginning of Part IV his ungainly posture in Samaniego's pharmacy is described with keen powers of observation and in very considerable detail. After his long absence from the centre of the stage it seemed important to Galdós to stress once more his abnormal physique. The positions he takes are reminiscent of a double-jointed, insect-like creature:

A veces, las piernas, en cruz, subían por un tablero próximo hasta mucho más arriba de donde estaba la cabeza; a veces, una de ellas se metía dentro de la estantería baja, por entre dos garrafas de drogas. En los dobleces del cuerpo las rodillas juntábanse a ratos con el pecho, y una de las manos servía de almohada a la nuca. Ya se apoyaba en la mesa sobre el codo izquierdo, ya el sobaco derecho montaba sobre el respaldo de la silla, como si ésta fuera una muleta; ya, en fin, las piernas se extendían sobre la mesa, cual si fueran brazos. . . . y en tanto el libro cambiaba de disposición con aquellos extravagantes escorzos del cuerpo del lector. Tan pronto aparecía por arriba, sostenido en una sola mano, como agarrado con las dos, más abajo de donde estaban las rodillas . . . (IV, i, 1, p. 415)

How much weaker than Fortunata he is, and how physically repugnant to her, is strikingly expressed by the devastatingly frank comment she makes on how she would deal with Maxi if he attacked Juanito:

¿Ves cómo se coge un langostino y se le arrancan las patas y se le retuerce el corpacho y se le saca lo que tiene dentro? Pues así. (II, vii, 7, p. 279)

His intelligence, too, seems initially extremely limited and he is pitifully shy and apathetic. He is treated as a child by Doña Lupe and his brothers. Yet without in the least minimizing his shortcomings Galdós manages to create a very real sympathy for him by a narrative tone which is both frank and understanding.

We should now consider how authentic the presentation of

his medical, and in particular his psychological, condition is; this has been most recently and most fully discussed by Ullman and Allison *(42)*. Care must be exercised in treating characters as medical case-histories and in particular in speculating beyond what is given in the text. At the same time medical evidence can be very useful in elucidating, verifying or assessing the information provided. From the point of view of literary appreciation, the portraiture, both physiological and psychological, seems eminently plausible. A full psychological analysis is probably more appropriate to the course of his madness than to his background and early life. Thus, to attribute to him an Oedipus complex as a result of his mother's neglect and to see the assault on his money box in terms of an attack on the father-figure *(42*, pp. 9 and 13) seems to me to stray a long way from the data given in the book. The question of his madness will be the subject of a separate section later on; for the moment we are concerned with the early formulation of his character. The initial scene of his meeting with Fortunata and his determination to marry her has already been discussed.

As a consequence of his physical limitations, Maxi has developed his imaginative power to such an extent that he is in danger of losing touch with reality. His fixation on the cadets of the Military School he can see parading combines this propensity for fantasy with his burning desire to compensate for his inadequate body. His solitary prowling about the streets at night is an aspect of his timidity; unable to overcome his inhibitions with respectable women, he sets out to make respectable a woman he has less hesitation in approaching —and, for better or for worse, he lights on Fortunata. I say 'for better or for worse' since it is a moot point whether he is better off or not as a result of meeting Fortunata. His fantasies are such, we are told, that he is liable to land in Leganés —the Madrid lunatic asylum— as a result of them anyway. The fact that Leganés is where he ends up at the close of the novel is thus anticipated. Without the Fortunata experience he would have been no better off, therefore, and his mental development would have remained stifled. But we must not anticipate. The fact is, though, that the mere decision to redeem Fortunata produces a flowering of initiative, self-assurance and intelligence unsuspected in him.

At this stage the question arises of Maxi's virility. There has been some critical discussion about whether he is impotent or not. Against Ricardo Gullón (*14*, p. 221; *31*, pp. 150-1) Montesinos declares emphatically that he is not (*16*, II, p. 257); and Ullman and Allison concur (*42*, p. 12). Galdós does not tell us explicitly, partly as a result of his well-known reticence about sexual details (though not about themes of sexual morality) and partly because this is a realm in which only an all-knowing narrator could possibly penetrate. Doña Lupe expresses grave doubts about his potency in her tactless remark ' . . . por el lado de las mujeres no temo nada, francamente. Ni a ti te gusta eso, ni puedes, aunque te gustara' (II, ii, 5, p. 182), but she has no way of telling. Fortunata, who has, clearly denies from the start of their relationship any chance of his fathering a child. Moreover, an early draft of the manuscript speaks unequivocally of his impotence. Yet it is clear that Maxi is in a certain degree sexually motivated. It is implied, in the manuscript more clearly than in the final text, that on occasions he consorts with prostitutes, but obviously we cannot tell with what success. How far theory and practice part company is left in doubt; all we can say is that his sexual prowess is at best minimal. Moreover, it is quickly sublimated out of existence:

> De tal modo se sutilizaron los sentimientos del joven Rubín con aquel extraordinario amor, que éste le inspiraba no sólo las buenas acciones, el entusiasmo y la abnegación, sino también la delicadeza llevada *hasta la castidad*. Su naturaleza pobre no tenía exigencias; su espíritu las tenía grandes, y éstas eran las que más le apremiaban. (II, ii, 1, p. 173)

His preference for the more spiritual word *amar* over the direct and everyday word *querer* corresponds to the same urge in a young man Biblically described as 'enclenque de cuerpo y robusto de espíritu'. Of the vigour of his spiritual passion to regenerate Fortunata there is no doubt as he uncovers the sordid details of her past life, launches upon violent denunciations of Santa Cruz and sets out to teach her to read and write. His personality is transformed: he becomes more alert, more studious, more curious about literature, more capable of understanding French. Despite his occasional worries about whether Fortunata does or can love him, circumstances at first seem to favour him. After proposing to her, he has a stroke of luck and the inheritance from his aunt at Molina de Aragón solves his immediate financial problems. He finishes his studies and is given a situation in Samaniego's pharmacy. He has, too, less trouble than expected with his family. When his aunt discovers Maxi's plans, thanks to Olmedo's indiscreion, she is interrupted and mollified, in an excellent scene (II, iii, 1-2), by a financially successful visit from Torquemada. Juan Pablo is indifferent to the whole matter and Nicolás conceives for himself the rôle of spiritual redeemer. The latter's proposal to put Fortunata in Las Micaelas is welcomed by Maxi, who is worried only by the incongruous fear that Fortunata might take to the religious life. He has come to adopt a view of the universe which is not bounded by space and is without horizons, in striking contrast with Las Micaelas church which, as we have seen, little by little cuts out all view of the sky and the outside world. Maxi's aspirations are boundless and theoretical, detached from reality; the norms of Las Micaelas are totally lacking in imagination and restrictive of personal freedom. 'La loca de la casa', as Galdós calls the imagination in this novel and elsewhere, must be restrained but not denied. Moreover, in order to defend his position against all comers, Maxi takes a mathematically fatalist position, reminiscent of the determinist philosopher Spinoza: 'todo lo que debe pasar, pasa . . . y todo lo que debe ser, es'. Providence, he believes, intervenes in individual lives and in this he blindly reposes his trust:

> Le había entrado fe ciega en la acción directa de la Providencia sobre el mecanismo funcionante de la vida menuda. La Providencia dictaba no sólo la historia pública, sino también la privada. (II, iv, 8, p. 226)

From the moment of the marriage onwards, however, everything turns out calamitously. It is evident that the marriage was not consummated: on the wedding day he has such an acute migraine that he has to be doped that night with laudanum; and, as Galdós says unequivocally, on the second night:

> el pobre chico no se encontraba en aptitud de expresarle su desmedido amor de otro modo que por manifestaciones relacionadas exclusivamente con el pensamiento y con el corazón. Palabras ardientes, sin eco en ninguna concavidad de la máquina humana, impulsos de cariño propiamente ideales, y de aquí no salía, es decir, no podía salir. (II, vii, 5, p. 274)

As for Fortunata, 'le cuidaba como se cuida a un niño, y se había borrado de su mente la idea de que era un hombre . . .' (p. 273). Once

she has renewed her affair with Juanito, moreover, she treats Maxi
with such utter frigidity that it cannot fail to have a desolating
effect on him. 'Medios espirituales', charity and hard work are of
no avail: she does not even look at him. He is quickly overpowered
by jealousy, both because of outside comments and jeers and his
own observations. He nearly catches her out about Juanito's in-
capacity when the latter breaks his arm riding, and implores her,
without success, to tell him the truth. He tries to escape from the
situation by wanting to go to Molina de Aragón, as advised by his
doctor, Augusto Miquis, who declared emphatically that he should
never have married.

By the end of Part II, when he receives explicit information about
his wife's infidelity and the marriage breaks down, the ground has
been prepared for the development of his madness. He already shows
one characteristic reaction, an urge towards violence, by buying a
revolver and by confronting Juanito. Then follows a long pause in
which we do not see Maxi until well into Part III when Feijoo
broaches the question of a reconciliation. He has by then abjured
violence and adopted, as he explains to Feijoo, a highly spiritual
philosophy, which is remarkably suitable for Don Evaristo's plans:

> la desgracia me ha hecho a mí volver los ojos a las cosas que no se
> ven ni se tocan. Si no lo hubiera hecho así, me habría muerto ya
> cien veces. ¡Y si viera usted qué distinto es el mundo mirado
> desde arriba a mirado desde abajo! (III, iv, 9, p. 350)

His refusal to countenance any restoration echoes the famous reiterated *jamás* of Prim to any Bourbon restoration and was just as
ineffectual. Following the reconciliation Maxi attracts little attention,
only enough to show that all is far from well with him mentally or
physically. We shall see the outcome of his condition when we
discuss Maxi's madness in a later section.

a) *The clash of Fortunata and Jacinta*

The eventual encounter of the two female protagonists is of exceptional importance. It is the culmination of much which has gone before and is carefully integrated into a complex structure in which Mauricia *la dura* and Doña Guillermina are closely concerned.

When Fortunata meets Mauricia in Las Micaelas, she learns about Juanito's pursuit of her and hears with emotion the story of *el Pitusín*. The new friendship strengthens her conviction of her right to love Juanito. At the same time her admiration and envy of Jacinta is aroused by the chatter of Doña Manolita Reoyos and by seeing Jacinta during an official visit. The contrast between her own fertility and Jacinta's barrenness is already clearly drawn; she dreams of their changing places and, prophetically, of handing over a child to her rival. But her conscience, in the form of a lively but stern homily delivered to her by God, shows her disposed to do her best in her forthcoming marriage. Nevertheless the Micaelas experience, which was supposed to separate Fortunata from the temptations of the world, in fact brought her into close emotional contact with both her ex-lover and his envied wife.

It is Mauricia, moreover, who on the eve of her friend's wedding announces the frightening proximity of Juanito in the flat next to hers, confirming her earlier conviction that he would continue to pursue her. She stoutly recommends Fortunata to marry Maxi whether or not she decides to behave honourably: 'la que tiene un peine de marido tiene bula para todo' (II, vii, 2, pp. 265). On the same occasion Mauricia teaches her a superstition about buttons: if you find a white one with four holes (*aujeritos*) it means good luck, whereas a black one with three holes indicates bad luck. As Mauricia interprets it, her good fortune depends on her marrying Maxi. The omen recurs much later and prolongs Mauricia's influence after her death, when Fortunata comes upon a black button immediately after her vivid dream about Juanito (III, vii, 4), representing despair about renewing the affair. Then, shortly afterwards, she finds a white one, corresponding to Mauricia's conception of good luck, just before meeting Juanito again.

Mauricia's most significant intervention in Fortunata's life occurs in the fine dramatic scenes when she is on her deathbed. Not only does she provide the occasion for Fortunata to encounter both Jacinta and Doña Guillermina, but her own influence continues to be important. This influence, described as mysterious, inexplicable and diabolical, is evidently an aspect of her own nature, one of the instinctive strings pulling her heart in the direction society considers reprehensible. But Mauricia has her own agonized alternations between contrition and rebellion and gives accordingly conflicting advice to Fortunata. On the one hand, she counsels complete and immediate repentance and abandonment of all resentment of Jacinta; and at the same time —and this is an essential point— roundly asserts that her love for Juanito is not sinful:

> —Arrepiéntete, chica, y no lo dejes para luego. Vete arrepintiendo de todo, menos de querer a quien te sale de *entre ti*, que esto no es, como quien dice, pecado. No robar, no *ajumarse*, no decir mentiras; pero en el querer, ¡aire, aire!, y caiga el que caiga. Siempre y cuando lo hagas así, tu miajita de cielo no te la quita nadie. (III, vi, 1, p. 370)

Shortly afterwards, Fortunata coincides with Jacinta in the flat and is astounded and confused at seeing her. Faced with Jacinta's 'sonrisa angelical' and her kindly protection of Adoración, she feels inadequate and inferior. Galdós skilfully exploits the fact that Jacinta does not recognize Fortunata; she goes to sit next to her on the sofa, adding to Fortunata's confusion. Gradually the latter's fear turns to anger and her admiration to resentment; at the same time narration gives way to the presentation of her thoughts in direct speech. Once more, she tries to detract from Jacinta's merits ('Ya sabemos que tiene usted un sinfín de perfecciones. ¿A qué cacarearlo tanto?'). She remembers Jacinta's efforts to adopt the boy she thought was Fortunata's son, and imagines her own reactions if Adoración were her child, not Mauricia's. She consciously stokes her resentment, building up to a potential outburst of denunciation and passing from the formal *usted* to the insulting *tú*:

> Porque tú quitaste lo que era mío . . . y si Dios hiciera justicia, ahora mismo te pondrías donde yo estoy, yo donde tú estás, grandísima ladrona . . . (III, vi, 3, p. 376)

This fury anticipates what will happen in the second stage of their encounter but is here interrupted by a question from Jacinta and by the appearance of Severiana. Fortunata's reflexions are now inter-spersed with an account of Mauricia's condition. She examines Jacinta's clothes, showing her working-class dislike for hats (Villalonga had described her to Juanito as having reached the peak of elegance of wearing a hat, I, xi, 1) and envying her coat and skirt. She notes Jacinta's tact in not accompanying Adoración to see Mauricia, but immediately seeks to undermine it: ' ¡Qué remilgos estos! Cuando digo que me cargan a mí estas perfecciones . . . ¡Qué monas nos hizo Dios!' (pp. 376-7).

Fortunata is overwhelmed by the whole scene, alternating un-certainly, like Mauricia, between impulses to weep and to explode in fury. She ends by bursting into tears at the accumulated troubles which have beset her. When she returns that evening, Mauricia has reverted to being the wild unruly rebel once more and upbraids her for not attacking her rival. This attitude corresponds clearly to one of the opposing impulses felt by Fortunata herself. Put under sedation, however, Mauricia is once more concerned with salvation, with Fortunata's as well as her own, and prays for Fortunata to follow her to heaven. But, though now advocating sympathy with Jacinta, she still declares that it is no sin to love Juanito. The tearful idea of dying together is something of an anticipation of Fortunata's early death in remarkably similar circumstances. The next morning Fortunata meditates on her real vocation to be a working man's wife:

> Si es lo que a mí me gusta, ser obrera, mujer de un trabajador honradote que me quiera . . . (III, vi, 5, p. 383)

The three factors we have just seen —the building up of resentment, Mauricia's conflicting example of violence and remorse and her pride in being from the *pueblo*— are all present in her full confrontation with Jacinta which follows.

Jacinta enters with Doña Guillermina and Fortunata cannot escape. She expects them to go off together but Jacinta comes and sits next to her on the sofa. Curious about this unknown beauty, Jacinta proceeds to ask a series of inopportune questions: has she children? did she ever have any? how long has she been married? The result is that Fortunata declares herself, inarticulately enough, to have been married for five years —'Yo me casé antes que usted . . .', the 'marriage' concerned being with the other's husband! There follows more interior monologue full of jealous resentment and, as the narrator tells us, of the raw, sincere passion of the *pueblo*, increased after Jacinta leaves the room. When to Fortunata's surprise she returns, the latter is off her guard and cannot contain herself any longer:

> Verla y cegarse fue todo uno. No podía darse cuenta de lo que pasó. Obedecía a un empuje superior a su voluntad cuando se lanzó hacia ella con la rapidez y el salto de un perro de presa. Juntáronse, chocando en mitad del angosto pasillo. La prójima le clavó sus dedos en los brazos, y Jacinta la miró aterrada, como quien está delante de una fiera . . . Entonces vio una sonrisa de brutal ironía en los labios de la desconocida, y oyó una voz asesina que le dijo claramente:
> —Soy Fortunata. (III, vi, 5, pp. 384-5)

In her *brutal ironía*, *voz asesina* and, later, her *insolente dureza*, Fortunata is clearly following the example of Mauricia *la dura* in her frenzies.

The effect of the scene on Jacinta did not last long; the impact of this incident, unlike the next time they came into contact (III, vii, 3), is on Fortunata, who despite valiant attempts to justify herself, feels a tremendous burden of self-recrimination at having flouted Feijoo's counsel of moderation and let herself down. Her resentment and her envy still continue after she returns home. That night she dreams of escape but realises that she has nowhere to go; she cannot face Feijoo's reproaches.

The interview or 'confession' with Doña Guillermina after Mauricia's death (III, vi, 10) is the worst spiritual experience Fortunata ever had (see Eoff, *13*, p. 60). It serves to clarify her conscience and, apparently, to make her accept the demands of society. If she now has no dealings with Juanito, why harbour any rancour against Jacinta? In confessing her sins, she repeats almost verbatim the contrite words Mauricia uttered so recently:

> (Mauricia) Arrepiéntete de todo, chica, pero de todo. Somos muy malas . . ., tú no sabes bien lo malas que somos. (p. 373)

> (Fortunata) Es que yo soy muy mala; no sabe usted lo mala que soy. (p. 397)

Guillermina urges upon her the sublimity of sacrifice —the sacrifice she had never had the opportunity to make— a concept Fortunata understands very well since she has already imagined herself heroically nursing Maxi if he were to contract some hideous disease. Guillermina is able to perceive, platonically, 'la representación ideal que de sus propias acciones y sentimientos tenía aquella infeliz en su espíritu' (p. 398), and her message of renunciation is apparently convincing for the moment. The other influence on her —the dead Mauricia— remains powerful nonetheless.

There follows one of the most curious features of the whole novel: the fusing in Fortunata's mind of the figures of Doña Guillermina and Mauricia. Galdós's narrator disclaims any ability to elucidate it:

> ¿Cómo así, siendo una y otra personas tan distintas? Fuera lo que fuese, la simpatía misteriosa que le había inspirado Mauricia se pasaba a Guillermina. ¿Cómo, pues, se podían confundir la que se señaló por sus vergonzosas maldades y la santa señora que era la admiración del mundo? (p. 400)

Part of the explanation, evidently, lies in the turmoil of Fortunata's spirit; her hesitation between the two opposing impulses within her causes their champions to become confused. I would also suggest, however, that the two women are united by a spiritual aspiration, whether this be intuitive or reflexive, destructive or constructive, which contrasts with the purely economic or hierarchical values of Doña Lupe or the social conformity advocated by Feijoo. Galdós is a long way from the moral neutrality of a Taine ('vice and virtue are products like vitriol and sugar') but is equally far from purely social judgements of behaviour. It seems to me that, though he is fully conscious of its potentially explosive nature, Galdós treats passionate involvement with considerable sympathy, even when it is turned towards ends which are conventionally deemed evil.

The second interview with Doña Guillermina shows a very different Fortunata, who now asserts herself powerfully for the first time. Despite her humble manner and sense of inferiority on entering, she dominates the normally self-possessed Doña Guillermina, who is for once unable to cope with Fortunata's brutal honesty, disconcerted as she is by Jacinta's eavesdropping and overcome by a sense of sin at telling a lie. And what Fortunata proclaims is of crucial importance to Jacinta. While admitting a possible reservation present when she married —to have denied it absolutely would have been to deny her enduring love for Juanito— unwittingly Fortunata makes crystal clear to Jacinta both Juanito's lasting though sporadic obsession with her and his total responsibility for her situation. He sought her out and broke her marriage; he not only promised to marry her and left her with child, as Jacinta already knows, but was responsible for

her subsequent conduct: 'Yo no habría sido mala . . . si él no me
hubiera plantado en medio del arroyo con un hijo dentro de mí'
(III, vii, 2, p. 405). Moreover, she asserts categorically her own
personal superiority over Jacinta: 'Esposa que no tiene hijos, no es
tal esposa'. She begins to elaborate her 'idea' —'la pícara idea' of the
title of the chapter— displaying all the qualities of the people which
she shared with Mauricia, affirming instinct against reflexion ('Y ¿qué
saco de reflexionar? Mientras más reflexiono, peor', p. 407). Savage,
brutal passion against conventional morals, principles, civilization;
her 'sonrisa sarcástica' and 'expresivo alzar de hombros' recall
Mauricia's outbursts. When she learns that Jacinta is there, and
when the latter denounces Fortunata as a 'ladrona', Fortunata replies
with extreme violence: 'la ira, la pasión y la grosería del pueblo se
manifestaron en ella de golpe, con explosión formidable' (p. 408).
As she returns home she gives rein to the frantic and disorganized
monologue already discussed (p. 44 above), in which Guillermina
and Mauricia are confused. She also has a vivid and plausible dream
full of wishful thinking, in which she takes a long walk through
familiar Madrid streets. She notices a shop selling tubes, pipes and
taps —an obvious phallic symbol— and eventually comes upon Juanito
Santa Cruz, ruined and looking for a job as a tram conductor. Dominated by her utter discontent with her situation —she conceives a
bitter aversion for the whole Rubín family and thinks for a moment
of suicide— she meets Juanito the day after Arnáiz *el gordo*'s funeral.
As the affair is renewed, this time with discretion, Fortunata clings
to her idea, not yet fully elucidated, the consequences of which will
appear in the dénouement.

b) *The course of Maxi's madness*

There has been much speculation about the exact nature of Maxi's
madness, which according to his latest medical commentators
(*42*, pp. 10-17) is a case of paranoid schizophrenia. Insanity was
attributed in the nineteenth century largely to physiological or
hereditary factors. The former are certainly present in Maxi: his
physical inadequacies made him subject from adolescence to day-
dreaming, and they account for his tenuous grasp of reality. As for
the second, it has been suggested (*42*, p. 11) that congenital syphilis
may have caused his stunted physique, which may in turn have given

rise to his schizophrenia. What is most remarkable in his portrayal is that his madness in its acutest form depends directly on conditioning by Fortunata, whose presence highlights both his sexual inadequacy and the success of others. Galdós is thus aware of the dynamic non-organic nature of mental illness in an age when it was considered as essentially static and intractable. As we have seen, immediately after the reconciliation in Part III Maxi's mental and physical state worsens. He is ashamed of his puny physique, the jeering comments of by-standers when they go out for a walk together and Fortunata's carrying him as if he were a child (III, vi, 8, p. 391). He becomes pathologically suspicious of everyone around him. His rooted dislike of Feijoo corresponds to a feeling of jealousy, justified as it happens, of anyone who could be his wife's lover. His work is also affected; his memory fails him and he muddles prescriptions. And once the affair with Juanito has resumed, Maxi's mental condition deteriorates still further. Bouts of ineffectual violence alternate with symptoms of withdrawal, obsessive reading of abtruse philo-sophy, followed by further wild suspicions of persecution, in which he believes that Papitos, Doña Lupe, Fortunata and Ballester are all engaged in a plot to poison him. He conceives ideas of renunciation, dreams of death and of suicide pacts which offer an escape from a psychologically unacceptable situation. His delusions take grotesque and almost comic forms. The body he loathes he labels *la bestia*, and he marshals, to the great alarm of Fortunata and Doña Lupe, an imposing array of weapons —a knife and various types of poison— to kill *la bestia* and free the spirit it imprisons.

The intolerable thought of Fortunata's physical relations with another man and of the child they are likely to engender gives rise to another delusion, perhaps fostered initially by the drugs he was taking, which manages to eliminate the abhorred sexual element: he postulates a Messiah to be born of Fortunata but conceived by pure thought; he sees himself as St Joseph without, accordingly, any sexual rôle.

When he later thinks Fortunata is dead and becómes lucid once more, he understands clearly the reason for these delusions, hatched 'en el seno cerebral donde fermenta eso que llaman celos' (p. 480). As he explains to Fortunata regarding his death wish: 'Yo no encon-traba a tu pecado otra solución que la muerte, ahí tienes por qué me nació en la cabeza . . . aquella idea de la liberación, pretextos y triquiñuelas de la mente para justificar el asesinato y el suicidio.' He has an equally clear concept of *Mesianitis*:

> Era también una modificación cerebral de los celos. ¡El Mesías . . . tu hijo, el hijo de un padre que no era tu marido! Empezó por ocurrírseme que yo debía matarte a ti y a tu descendencia, y luego esta idea hervía y se descomponía como una sustancia puesta al fuego, y entre las espumas burbujeaba aquel absurdo del Mesías. Examínalo bien, y verás que todo era celos, celos fermentados y en putrefacción. (IV, vi, 3, p. 508)

Once, however, his intuition of Fortunata's pregnancy has precipitated her departure, he largely recovers from these extraordinary aberrations, not as a result of the savage 'Scottish showers' or hydrotherapy given him as treatment, for Galdós, through his medical contacts, was well aware of their uselessness. The reason for his recuperation is the removal of its immediate cause; as Quevedo graphically put it: '*Muerto el perro, se acabó la rabia*' (p. 490). His abnormal intellectual astuteness subsists nonetheless. By the exercise of pure logic he refutes the story of Fortunata's death and systematically discovers where she lives and her circumstances and is easily able to interpret the transparently clear message ('la pájara mala sacó pollo esta mañana', p. 497) which *Doña Desdémona* sends to Doña Lupe about the birth of the baby. Finally he discloses Juanito's affair with Aurora to his wife and thus causes her to give the decisive final twist to the plot.

In the evolution of his psychosis Maxi is brought into comparison with four other characters who serve to clarify his motives and attitudes: a device of literary technique which reveals how incomplete any purely medical case history must be. First, an argument with Torquemada marks the height of insane speculation he has reached in formulating his spiritual philosophy. Maxi claims to have discovered the formula he was seeking —not the money-spinning 'panacea' Doña Lupe is so eager for— but on the problem of the emanation of souls. He picks up Torquemada's favourite word 'materialismo' and roundly denounces the usurer and Juan Pablo as materialists. The episode convinces his aunt and wife that he is insane beyond recall.

Second, he has an encounter, after Fortunata's disappearance, with José Ido, whom he had earlier met discoursing learnedly on the

French Revolution and the need for balance between freedom and order. Ido is subject to one of his attacks, the result of eating meat (pellagra-induced, according to medical sources, *42*, p. 15) and raves about his purely imaginary loss of honour to the real cuckold Maximiliano. 'Los que tenemos la desgracia de ser esposos de una adúltera . . ., los que tenemos esa desgracia, no podemos responder de aquel mandamiento que dice: *no matar*. Creo que es el quinto' (IV, v, 2, p. 491). This cannot fail to strike Maxi to the quick as he replies: '—Sí, el quinto es— dijo Maxi, que sentía una corriente fría pasándole por el espinazo.' And, like Maxi himself earlier in the novel, Ido received no sympathy or understanding from other people; only Maxi encourages him from his own experience since Ido's aberration enables him to see clearly his own situation even if he mistakes the treatment:

> Don José, a usted le convendría tomar duchas y también unas pildoritas de bromuro de sodio. ¿Quiere que se las prepare? Es el tratamiento más eficaz para combatir eso . . . Dígamelo usted a mí, que durante una temporada he estado como usted . . ., muchísimo peor. Yo inventaba religiones; yo quería que todo el género humano se matara; yo esperaba el Mesías . . . Pues aquí me tiene tan sano y tan bueno . . . (p. 491)

Tan sano y tan bueno? He certainly appears so on the surface to those around him, but nonetheless they have their doubts. Fortunata: '¿este hombre está cuerdo o cómo está? Eso que dice, ¿es razón, o los mayores disparates que en mi vida le he oído?' (IV, vi, 3, p. 508); Ballester: 'Yo no me fío de la cordura de este caballerito, y siempre que le cojo a mano le registro, a ver si trae algún arma' (IV, vi, 8, p. 521); Guillermina: 'Lo último que me ha dicho es el colmo de la sabiduría y de la cordura; pero . . .' (p. 523).

Third, the question of intrinsic goodness is raised with Doña Guillermina, who is confused about what attitude to take towards him. After praising her sanctity, Maxi indicates that he has overcome passions and endured suffering such as we know Guillermina has never experienced:

> Primero tuve el delirio persecutorio; después, el delirio de grandezas . . . Inventé religiones; me creí jefe de una secta que había de transformar el mundo. Padecí también furor de homicidio, y por poco mato a mi tía y a *Papitos*. Siguieron luego depresiones horribles, ganas de morirme, manía religiosa, ansias de anacoreta y el delirio de la abnegación y el desprendimiento . . . (p. 522)

Yet the inexorable quest for justice and goodness and the calculated rationality in informing Fortunata of Aurora's treachery so that she should punish herself in exemplary fashion are, as Guillermina suspects, too inhuman to be quite sane. The doubts of the various characters who surround him are fully justified.

One more incident is to disturb his fragile equilibrium. When he implacably maintains that Fortunata has simply fostered Aurora's liaison with Juanito by her violence, his wife fastens on his weak point, calling him a man without honour and offering to love him passionately if he will kill the two lovers. Faced with this challenge, Maxi's calm collapses in a last bout of violent behaviour, followed by an extenuating lethargy. Once he is convinced of his wife's death, he reverts to his previous withdrawn serenity, but what now faces him is confinement in an asylum. As an inmate of Leganés, has he any hopes of recovery? Certainly not as a result of treatment there, for, as Galdós well knew (*42*, pp. 20-2), Leganés had no claim to be a therapeutic hospital, but perhaps a voluntary withdrawal into a world of meditation was the best course for him.

Maxi's final encounter is with Segismundo, who in a similar way exalts the dead Fortunata as an angel, but without the complete escape from the material world which constitutes Maxi's madness: 'usted está aun atado a las sinrazones de la vida; yo me liberté, y vivo en la pura idea' (p. 547). It only remains to speculate on whether the traumatic experience of his marriage to Fortunata was as unmitigated a disaster as most critics have assumed. Certainly it had no basis in reality, as Maxi admitted:

> Hice de ella el objeto capital de mi vida, y ella no respondió a mis deseos . . . No contamos con la Naturaleza, que es la gran madre y maestra que rectifica los errores de sus hijos extraviados . . . (IV, vi, 16, pp. 546-7)

Yet if it brought him untold anguish, his love for her stimulated in him a mental development which, though obsessive, abnormal and even insane, might be thought superior to the stunted, mediocre life he led before he met her. In a certain way, through her and with the idealized recollection of her after her death, he has found his solution.

c) *Resolution of conflicts*

Galdós begins the final part of *Fortunata y Jacinta* by introducing a new quite major character who is of substantial importance for the working out of the story. Segismundo Ballester, the chemist in charge of the Samaniego pharmacy, is suitably characterized by distinctive external traits: dishevelled appearance, abrupt and abrasive tone, and sardonic wit, and he is allowed considerable independent development, especially in his relationship with Olimpia's boy-friend, the critic Ponce. His importance, however, lies in his dealings with Maxi, as we have seen, and more particularly with Fortunata. He does not conceal his love for her but makes no demands, acting at all times, both before the break with Juanito and after she returns to La Cava de San Miguel, as a loyal and trusted friend. It is he whom everyone relies upon before and after the birth of Juan Evaristo. He is quite prepared to lose his job on her account and does so after the attack on Aurora. At her death he is distraught and kisses her face for the first time. He insists on buying a tombstone for her and Guillermina dissuades him only with difficulty from paying for her funeral. Altogether, Ballester represents an effective tribute to Fortunata's personal qualities. Though fully aware of her past life, he has no doubt about her intrinsic worth: for him also she is an 'ángel a su manera'.

After the funeral he recovers his balance. He is sad at the thought of his memory of her fading, but realizes the danger of his deep infatuation. His last service is to take his friend Maxi, who shares with him an idealistic love for the dead imperfect angel, to see her grave and to accompany him to the asylum.

Another essentially new character of the fourth part is Aurora Samaniego (she had been fleetingly mentioned in II, iv, 2, as a possible wife for Juan Pablo Rubín). She has less individual development but is of the greatest functional significance. The widow of a Frenchman killed in the Franco-Prussian War, ex-mistress of Moreno-Isla, an independent business woman and manageress of a new fashion shop, and the particular friend and confidante of Fortunata, she is pretentious, slanderous and treacherous. For each of the principal characters except Maxi she has a decisive relevance: it is she who puts into Fortunata's head the idea that Jacinta is having an affair with Moreno-Isla; later, she suggests that Segismundo Ballester is the father of Fortunata's baby; and she is the secret lover of Juanito, and consequently the cause of Fortunata's death.

The suggestion that Jacinta might be unfaithful has a profound effect on Fortunata. If Jacinta fails, then all moral standards crumble, and she is no worse than Jacinta or anyone else: '¡Ya no había virtud! ¡Ya no había más ley que el amor! . . . ¡Ya podía ella alzar su frente! Ya no le sacarían ningún ejemplo que la confundiera y abrumara. Ya Dios las había hecho a todas iguales . . . para poderlas perdonar a todas' (IV, i, 12, p. 444). By broaching the question to Juanito, Fortunata gave him a pretext for starting to break their relations once more. Meanwhile, she herself remains in agonizing uncertainty, an uncertainty Aurora does nothing to dispel.

> Es que si no fuera honrada esa mujer [she declares] a mí me parecería que no hay honradez en el mundo y que cada cual puede hacer lo que le da la gana . . . Paréceme que se rompe todo lo que la ata a una; no sé si me explico; y que ya lo mismo da blanco que negro. (IV, iii, 2, p. 466)

In her reflections once she has moved back to La Cava, she is still madly inquisitive about Jacinta's honour, but it is not until she questions Doña Guillermina after her baby is born that she is convinced that the alleged affair with Moreno-Isla is no more than Aurora's malice.

The second issue in which Aurora is involved is, of course, her secret affair with Juanito. She has promised to find out for Fortunata who the new lover was, but kept away from her at the time of Juan Evaristo's birth. When Maxi tells her of Aurora's treachery, she has an access of fury similar to that in which she attacked Jacinta, and which lasts in a latent state through visits by Ballester and Guillermina until she goes out and savagely assaults Aurora: in deed and word she reveals 'toda la pasión y la grosería' of the 'mujer del pueblo', worthy of Mauricia in her most violent moments. Her abhorrence of Aurora is caused by the treachery perpetrated on both the women who in their different ways have a claim on Juanito, to which is added her outrage at Aurora as a 'calumniadora' who has falsely accused Jacinta of adultery. Her thirst for revenge does not end here, for she incites Maxi to kill her and Juanito and reacts furiously, immediately before she has her fatal haemorrhage, when she learns of Aurora's second slander: that Ballester was the father of Juan Evaristo.

The attack on Aurora is at once a powerful reminder that

Fortunata possesses the violent passions of the people and a stage in the reconciliation with Jacinta. The fact that Juanito evidently had a new lover was something which brought them together even before she knew who their rival was: 'Y ahora estamos las dos de un color. A ninguna de las dos nos quiere. Estamos lucidas . . . Ambas nos podríamos consolar . . .' (IV, iv, 1, p. 482). At the same time in her improved manners and powers of expression, conspicuous now that she has returned to her old haunts, she feels socially on more equal terms with Jacinta. Moreover, on the purely natural plane she has the incomparable superiority of having a child by Juanito: 'Yo soy madre del único *hijo de la casa* . . . yo lo que quiero es que conste, que conste, sí, que una servidora es la madre del heredero, y que sin una servidora no tendrían nieto' (IV, vi, 2, pp. 504-5). This is the culmination of her idea, cherished for so long, and which represents one of the unifying threads running through much of the novel.

The preoccupation with Jacinta remains after the assault on Aurora: she wants ardently to count not only on her forgiveness but on her friendship. This urge towards reconciliation culminates in a final *rasgo* —one which, despite Feijoo's counsels, is not to be repented of —that of leaving her baby to Jacinta; it brings about the posthumous satisfaction of the *abrazo* of friendship Jacinta imagines giving her.

Her death scene deliberately recalls that of Mauricia earlier on (see Hafter, *15*, p. 236), though Fortunata's is presented directly and in more detail. Mauricia's last moments were seen through Doña Lupe's sceptical eyes, and it is not clear whether the last word she uttered was 'más [jerez] ' or 'ya. Como quien dice: "Ya veo la gloria y los ángeles" ' (III, vi, 9, p. 393). In other words, whether she died with her mind on spiritual or material things. Fortunata's death is similarly ambiguous.

As Estupiñá observes when she has finished dictating the letter to Jacinta, she revives only at the mention of Juanito, not at the thought of religion, and he makes a remark which links her directly to Mauricia: 'Es como los borrachos, que aunque estén expirando, si les nombran vino, parece que resucitan' (IV, vi, 14, p. 538). At her moment of death, the same Father Nones —a significantly negative name— receives no clear repentance and comments: 'No ha podido

confesar —Cabeza trastornada . . . ¡Pobrecita! Dice que es ángel. . .
Dios lo verá' (p. 541). But if there is no official confession, we
can hardly doubt that the unofficial one administered by Doña
Guillermina had its validity for the purposes of determining our
final attitude to the heroine. After receiving Jacinta's thanks and
forgiveness, she pardons Juanito without effort and Aurora with
great reluctance, but she does not renounce what Guillermina calls
'una idea maligna, origen de muchos pecados' (p. 540) that because
she had his children she was morally married to Juanito. Her idea,
tenaciously sustained and elaborated throughout the book and
supported by Mauricia, is never denied: the 'natural love' on which
her life is based is defended to the end. She simply declares that she
is an angel and, equating herself with Jacinta, 'también . . . *mona del
cielo*'. There is no doubt to my mind that despite the absence of
official approbation, this honest consistency on which her life has
been based signifies that in the eyes of her creator she died in the
odour of sanctity; or in the terms employed in the novel, as an
angel.

As for Jacinta, the poignant episode of Moreno-Isla's despair and
death in the second chapter of Part IV is essentially concerned with
her, though Galdós gives it an extended treatment which has also
religious and existential implications. His hopeless love for Jacinta
causes the emotional turbulence which is at the root of his illness.
He cannot make up his mind whether or not to return to England,
and envies beggars in the street their peace of mind and Guillermina
her sense of vocation. He inquires of his doctor whether he is
capable of having children but in all the time he and Jacinta have
been together he is never bold enough to make advances to her; and
he is mortally hurt when she fails to comment to Guillermina on his
new attempts at piety. For her part, though well disposed to him,
she shows herself not unaware of his love by not taking seriously
Doña Bárbara's fatuous efforts to marry him to her younger sister.

Little is seen of Jacinta towards the end of the book, but her
final reactions are important. We are not told of the effect the
birth of Fortunata's baby had on her, but it is clear that Doña
Guillermina, who unilaterally and with great aplomb declares herself tutor of the infant appointed by God, also has her idea: she is
working on Jacinta's behalf to secure the child for her if and when

opportunity arises. We do learn though that Jacinta approved of Fortunata's assault on Aurora, which to her mind redeems part of the sins of Juanito's first lover.

In her final appearance in the novel, after decisively spurning her husband, she endows the newly-adopted baby with her husband's features but with the heart of Moreno-Isla: 'aquel corazón que la adoraba y que se moría por ella' (IV, vi, 15, p. 544). He should have been her husband, she muses, with Juanito's charming face, or without it. At the end of the novel Jacinta has come to realize that the world is by no means as it ought ideally to be and to cease to respect as inviolable the laws of society: 'también ella tenía su idea respecto a los vínculos establecidos por la ley, y los rompía con el pensamiento . . . ' (p. 544): like Fortunata, she has come to concede that there are human passions which cannot be contained within the rigidly, divinely-ordained pattern sustained by Doña Guillermina.

The source of all the complex troubles, Juanito, is dispatched peremptorily. He is finally called to account: 'Había faltado gravemente, ofendiendo a su mujer legítima, abandonando después a su cómplice, y haciendo a ésta digna de compasión y aun de simpatía, por una serie de hechos de que él era exclusivamente responsable' (p. 543). Jacinta, who had earlier (IV, vi, 10, p. 529) begun to show a certain impatience at his demands for attention, now demonstrates a new determination, a loss of affection, and above all open contempt for him such as she had not revealed before. Deprived of his self-esteem, he starts to experience the effects of having suffered an irreparable loss, of aging while still young, of loneliness within a family. An appropriate enough ending to his irresponsible behaviour and an artistically satisfying one which is in some ways reminiscent of certain of Cervantes's *Novelas ejemplares*,[24] it might seem somewhat unrealistic in view of the undisputed male dominance of nineteenth-century society.

In Chapter V another story is brought to its conclusion. Juan Pablo Rubín, at the very moment when he is proclaiming the most

[24]I am thinking of Loaysa in *El celoso extremeño*, who, when Leonor enters a convent after her husband's death, 'despechado y casi corrido, se pasó a las Indias'.

radical of revolutionary positions as a result of his failure to enlist his aunt's help in meeting his pressing debts, is, like his brother Nicolás, honoured by Villalonga, on Feijoo's recommendation, with a most unmerited appointment. This most fickle and superficial of café philosophers thus becomes the governor of a province (a third-class one, to be sure); the loser turns out to be his mistress Refugio, who is promptly discarded.

Maxi had been thrown off course in his philosophy of cold abstract reason by Fortunata's offer to love him passionately if he killed Aurora and Juanito. Ballester is only able to persuade him that his wife is dead by taking her to see her grave where the stone he had commissioned was now in place. (There they fail to see the funeral procession of Don Evaristo Feijoo which brings to a conclusion one more aspect of the story.) After copious weeping, Maxi sums up his mistakes:

> La quise con toda mi alma. Hice de ella el objeto capital de mi vida, y ella no respondió a mis deseos. No me quería ... Miremos las cosas desde lo alto: no me podía querer. Yo me equivoqué, y ella también se equivocó. No fui yo sólo el engañado: ella también lo fue. Los dos nos estafamos recíprocamente. (IV, vi, 16, pp. 546-7)

With her death, 'el mundo acabó para mí'. His madness, he declares, 'mis extravíos, ¿qué han sido más que la expresión exterior de las agonías de mi alma?' Fortunata has now been transformed into an ideal, a free spirit no longer subject to the 'asquerosidades de la realidad': an angel. In this state of mind he claims to live in the pure idea, and though he realizes that he is being taken to Leganés, he makes no objection, since his mind is free: 'No encerrarán entre murallas mi pensamiento. Resido en las estrellas. Pongan al llamado Maximiliano Rubín en un palacio o en un muladar ... Lo mismo da' (p. 548).

Galdós has chosen to end his longest novel with the words of Maximiliano Rubín, the most independent and original of the characters in the book. The words themselves reflect a clear sublimation of material and physical considerations which have brought him and could only bring him anguish and bitter disappointments. His mental development has been very considerable and his rational powers are very acute, yet there is little doubt that they are used in so obsessive a way as to constitute madness. In a country and in a language in which the supreme literary creation is an inspired madman, there is nothing too surprising about that. What is remarkable is that Maximiliano is perhaps second only to Don Quixote as a highly sympathetic study of madness in Spanish literature.

VII Conclusion

Fortunata y Jacinta has awakened a variety of responses. Some critics, like John Rutherford for example, consider Galdós's vision to be basically optimistic, in which 'society emerges . . . as one large and —on the whole— happy family' (*8*, p. 293). Similarly, for Nimetz, 'this novel, more than any other by Galdós, leaves the impression that people are sane, healthy, honest, and good' (*17*, p. 187); it is, with two exceptions, 'less critical of society than any of the others' (p. 192), 'reflects the social ideal of universal charity' (p. 194) and takes on 'some of the glow of a fairy tale' (p. 196). Much more moderate is Sherman Eoff's statement: 'His is unquestionably an optimistic philosophy, but it is free from sentimentalism and complacency' (*23*, p. 146). In sharp contrast, Anthony Zahareas emphasizes the tragic impact of the novel:

> The tragic sense of the novel is developed around the suffering and destruction of individuals in their attempt to remake contradictory but desired goods. Galdós never once resolved the opposites. (*27*, p. 46)

Casalduero, too, inclines towards a pessimistic interpretation, seeing Guillermina's charity as the only bright spot:

> lo único que hallan todos es el vacío, la nada de la vida. La tierra es lugar de sufrimiento y dolor, lugar de servidumbre . . . Pero en la tierra, lugar de desolación y de tristeza hay una llama viva, la caridad ardiente de Guillermina. (*9*, pp. 110-11)

The critics are no less divided on its ideology. Various scholars, led by Stephen Gilman (*40,41;30,31*) see the novel as the working out of a complex mythological pattern, while others (Blanco Aguinaga, *36*, Sinnigen, *39*, Rodríguez Puértolas, *38*) view it as a social document. Others have drawn attention to its deep immersion in history and contemporary events (*2, 12, 37*). Galdós has been accused of a reprehensible complacency (*3*, pp. 191-236) or of not taking his own work seriously (*8*, p. 296). In the face of such extraordinary diversity, let us attempt to establish certain general conclusions.

First of all, the question of Galdós's alleged bland optimism. This approach is to my mind largely conditioned by an uncritical acceptance of the narrative tone as Galdós's own attitude. What seem to me significant are the many occasions when Galdós shows himself extremely conscious of the untapped or ignored potential in human existence. In this respect the death of Moreno-Isla transcends the importance it has in Jacinta's story. He provides an example, not only of extreme frustration and waste of human talent ('lo que se desea no se tiene nunca', p. 452) but also —despite the futility of his own individual existence— of the continual renewal of life:

> Se desprendió de la Humanidad, cayó del gran árbol la hoja completamente seca, sólo sostenida por fibra imperceptible. El árbol no sintió nada en sus inmensas ramas. Por aquí y por allí caían en el mismo instante hojas y más hojas inútiles; pero la mañana próxima había de alumbrar innumerables pimpollos, frescos y nuevos. (IV, ii, 6, p. 461)

Waste and yet renewal: a balance, then, between the extremes of pessimism and optimism.

The criticism of superficiality about society is also largely unjustified. The various instances of the lack of human sympathy indicated in the course of this study reveal a far from self-satisfied attitude towards the community. Maxi, José Ido, Mauricia *la dura*, Papitos and Segismundo Ballester all suffer in various ways from harsh and undeserved treatment at the hands of others. No less disturbing to complacency are the unmerited fates which afflict Fortunata and to a lesser extent Jacinta as a result of Juanito's perfidy, or the anguish endured by Maxi as a result of his misplaced idealism. These hardships have their counterparts in the equally unjust rewards bestowed on Juan Pablo and Nicolás Rubín, as a direct result of Fortunata's misconduct, as she herself observes:

> Si no hubiera sido por mi maldad, ¡cuándo habría sido canónigo este tonto de capirote, ordinario y hediondo! (III, vi, 7, p. 388)

A judgement which is confirmed by Doña Lupe:

> ¡Dar una canonjía a un clérigo joven, que entra en su casa a la una de la noche y pasa el tiempo charlando en el café con los curas de caballería que andan por ahí sueltos y sin licencias! (III, v, 1, p. 358)

The end of the novel witnesses the tragic death of a young woman in her prime, a loss emphasized by the depth of Ballester's and Maxi's grief, and the apparently irreversible insanity of Maxi himself. Yet the principal impact is not cathartic but leaning rather towards renewal and reconciliation. The main example of course is found in the two heroines who gradually draw together as Fortunata's admiration for the honourable status of her rival grows and as Jacinta becomes more and more aware (the attack on Aurora serving as a catalyst) of Fortunata's passionate sincerity. Fortunata's death leaves behind her a solution to Jacinta's problem as well as a deepened awareness. Jacinta, for so long a devoted admirer of Doña Guillermina, now attains a new consciousness of the complex ambiguity of human life:

> También ella tenía su idea respecto a los vínculos establecidos por la ley, y los rompía con el pensamiento, realizando la imposible obra de volver el tiempo atrás, de mudar y trastrocar las calidades de las personas, poniendo a éste el corazón de aquél, y a tal otro la cabeza del de más allá, haciendo, en fin, unas correcciones tan extravagantes a la obra total del mundo, que se reiría de ellas Dios si las supiera, y su vicario con faldas, Guillermina Pacheco. Jacinta hacía girar todo este ciclón de pensamientos y correcciones alrededor de la cabeza angélica de Juan Evaristo; recomponía las facciones de éste, atribuyéndole las suyas propias, mezcladas y confundidas con las de un ser ideal, que bien podría tener la cara de Santa Cruz, pero cuyo corazón era seguramente el de Moreno . . ., aquel corazón que la adoraba y que se moría por ella . . . Porque bien podría Moreno haber sido su marido . . ., vivir todavía, no estar gastado ni enfermo, y tener la misma cara que tenía el *Delfín*, ese falso, mala persona . . . 'Y aunque no la tuviera, vamos, aunque no la tuviera . . . ¡Ah!, el mundo entonces sería como debía ser, y no pasarían las muchas cosas malas que pasan . . .' (IV, vi, 15, p. 544)

Maxi's confinement in Leganés is likewise neither entirely tragic nor smug: it is a tranquil acceptance of the inevitable.

Although the claims made that the novel has a thoroughgoing symbolic or mythological structure on the basis of bird-imagery seem to me exaggerated, it has, undoubtedly, a firm structure in which certain motifs —fertility versus sterility, 'revolution' versus 'restoration' of legality, spontaneity versus conformity, etc.— recur again and again throughout the book. There are also frequent interactions (influences, complementary interventions, contrasts) of great structural importance: we have seen the impact of Feijoo, Mauricia and Guillermina on Fortunata, of Moreno-Isla on Jacinta, of José Ido on Maxi, as well as the obsessive relationship, at first distant but gradually drawing closer physically and spiritually, between the two heroines. The psychological development stressed by Sherman Eoff (*13*; *23, 24*), by which both Fortunata and Maxi adjust to varying circumstances, is likewise remarkably skilful.

The interpretation of contemporary history and the action of the novel is also very substantial, so that, even if the events concerned are less momentous than those of *Le Rouge et le Noir* and *War and Peace*, *Fortunata y Jacinta* still conforms exactly to Wellek's statement: 'In some writers, but not all, realism becomes historic: it grasps social reality as dynamic evolution' ('The Concept of Realism', p. 253).

I have already discussed the question of Galdós's ironic quasi-identification with the bourgeoisie (pp. 37-42). It is quite clear that there is no question of Galdós's hating the bourgeoisie with the virulence which characterizes Flaubert and other French writers, but this does not mean that he foregoes any critical attitude. His essential concern, however, is not with a critique of society as such, but with the shifting relationship between the individual and the community in which he lived. As Sherman Eoff has indicated:

> In this novel, Galdós, with no particular thesis to preach, gives perhaps his most vigorous depiction of social movement; and it must be emphasized that he does so by way of a study of personal adjustments more than he does by external description of the social system. (*13*, p. 101)

A clear contrast is drawn between those who accept society's values and opportunities without question —the Santa Cruz family, Doña Lupe, even Severiana— and those who through passion, ambition or frustration rebel against its rules or conventions. The shallowest of the rebels are Juan Pablo Rubín and Izquierdo who fulminate against the system only until they are comfortably incorporated into it. To some extent Doña Guillermina emerges from her class and pursues her own ideal; it is to this point positive, even though circumscribed by her own limited perspective. In contrast, the dissatisfaction of her nephew Moreno-Isla is never assuaged. Jacinta's constant frustration produced an inner rebellion and finally a certain understanding of the injustices of the world ('lo desarregladas que andan las cosas del mundo').

Don Evaristo Feijoo, too, has a clear insight into how society functions, and conforms only nominally, just as Juanito, far more callously and cynically, does. But Feijoo's conciliatory tactics inevitably cause injustices and cannot in the event curb the *rasgos* or passionate outbursts of his protégée. For her part, Fortunata is never fully convinced of the value of restraining her spontaneous impulses. In the end, she earns tacit approval for her assault upon Aurora, and her final *rasgo* of passing her baby son to Jacinta shows that such instinctive actions have their positive side. Mauricia's rebellion is deeper and more mysterious; it is linked with repressed spiritual aspirations and not simply with personal ambition. The identification established with Doña Guillermina in Fortunata's mind shows that the two women, so different in way of life, have something in common: a similar spiritual yearning.

The character with the deepest grounds for discontent —Maximiliano Rubín— turns in his anguish alternately outward (towards murdering his wife and her lover) and inward (towards suicide, a philosophy of renunciation, withdrawal). Exceptionally, among the characters, the wrongs inflicted on him cause a personal not a social reaction; he does not vent his spleen on others and he is sympathetic to a fellow-sufferer like Ido. His implacable sense of justice is however more than humanly realistic and serves only to set Fortunata's primitive passions on fire once more. His philosophical speculations are far removed from society's ambitions and quarrels: hence his voluntary separation from the world in the concluding words of the book.

Much of the above demonstrates how careful we should be in taking the terms of conventional moral praise or condemnation at their face value. As Monroe Z. Hafter says of another novel: 'Galdós patently sets out to demonstrate that good cannot be neatly separated from evil' (*15*, p. 239). Time and time again Doña Guillermina and Jacinta are referred to as 'santa' or 'ángel', while Mauricia is categorized as 'satánica', 'diabla', 'mujer mala', etc. and so, frequently, is Fortunata, until her aspirations to be an 'ángel' like Jacinta come to be considered. In considering this contrast between *angelismo* and *diabolismo* reiterated throughout the book, it is wise to recall the cautionary note struck by Gustavo Correa:

> Los conceptos del bien y del mal aparecen unas veces como categorías discernibles e incambiables, pero otras veces quedan sometidos a este movimiento ondulatorio que borra fronteras

absolutas y los sitúa en una zona de relatividad. (*11*, p. 102)

Several discussions take place about saintliness, with reference to Doña Guillermina. Doña Lupe can hardly distinguish between true charity and social climbing, but Maxi can and does aspire in all humility to be saintly and, unlike the *santa y fundadora*, as a result of great anguish; more modestly, Ballester acts without fuss as a completely devoted friend. Nor should the innate wickedness of Mauricia, much less that of Fortunata, be too readily assumed (see p. 78). What is clear to me is that for Galdós those who dispense disinterested sympathy or assistance with genuine compassion are morally superior to those who are more calculating in their charity.

It is clear that official standards of charity differ markedly from genuine moral ones, however elusive or ambiguous the latter may be. Though fully conscious of the hazards involved, I venture to put forward certain tentative suggestions towards distinguishing a true scale of values. Maxi, Ballester and Fortunata, as prodigal in her generosity as she is vehement in her hatred, must stand at the highest level, above Jacinta and Feijoo, who are more selective or prudent in their commitment to other people. These in turn show a compassion which is not invariably apparent in the 'official' saint Guillermina. Mauricia and Moreno-Isla, in very different ways, also display real though sporadic impulses of concern for others. Don Baldomero and Doña Barbàrita are benevolent and charitable but it costs them no effort and they are quite oblivious of anything outside their immediate world. A lower category will comprise characters where personal interest weighs at least as much as beneficence: Doña Casta, Juan Pablo Rubín and, of course, Doña Lupe. Finally come. the figures who have no sense of compassion at all: Nicolás Rubín, Torquemada, Aurora and, above all, Juanito.

The means by which Galdós's much discussed ambiguity[25] expresses itself most clearly is irony.[26] Irony lends to the text a

[25] An interesting case for the deliberate ambiguity of *Nazarín* has recently been made by Peter Goldman, supported by Brian Dendle (*AG*, IX (1974), 99-112, 113-21).

[26] For a thorough discussion of types of irony, see D. C. Muecke, *The Compass of Irony* (London, 1969), and the same author's book *Irony* (The Critical Idiom, 13, London, 1970).

breadth of interpretations which defy simple analysis. Cosmic irony, with tragic implications, is evident in the situations we have examined of Maxi, Ido and Moreno-Isla. Ironies of situation abound. One may cite as representative examples Doña Barbarita's fears in the very first chapter that Juanito would be exploited by unscrupulous women; the death of Isabel Cordero at the peak of achievement at pulling off Jacinta's ideal marriage, which, ironically, turned out badly; Jacinta's barrenness contrasted with her mother's and her sisters' fecundity; Feijoo's meeting Fortunata so late in life and his prudently conducted yet rash affair with her; Aurora in her hypocritical dual rôle as Fortunata's confidante and Juanito's lover. On a smaller scale, too, such ironies occur in plenty: Jacinta remembers vaguely that some 'marimorena' occurred at Sagunto (I, v, 4, p. 57) –the siege by Hannibal in 218 B.C.!– thus anticipating the *pronunciamiento* which will restore the Bourbons three years later. The winner of the lottery (I, x, 1) has to be such an opulent gentleman as Baldomero Santa Cruz. Maxi caps the self-conscious bohemian ways of Olmedo by actually marrying a prostitute. Doña Lupe assumes that Fortunata is pregnant (improbably foreseeing 'la probable reproducción del tipo de Rubín en la especie humana', p. 386) when she feels unwell after the confrontation with Jacinta (III, vi, 6).

Some situations lend themselves particularly to an ironic treatment full of incongruity and *socarronería*: Maxi's breaking his money box and the preparations for Mauricia to receive the Viaticum, as we have seen; Doña Lupe persuading herself of the morality of assisting Fortunata –whose money she holds– despite her adultery (IV, iii, 5).

Many of the verbal ironies depend on the narrative technique. Guillermina, *virgen y fundadora*, is referred to as having *ciento y pico de hijos de uno y otro sexo* (I, vii, 1, p. 76). When Nicolás draws close to Fortunata during their first interview, the narrator hastens to point out that the cleric's taste for *carne* is confined to the edible kind; his command to fumigate the house (*sahumar*) after Fortunata's infidelity is just as applicable to him (many other instances concerning Nicolás might be cited). Izquierdo's garbled comments on historical figures are received with disdainful glances by the porter from the Academy of History and are then followed by Ido's ultra-simplified (though factually accurate) account of the

French Revolution (IV, v, 1, p. 488). Altogether, Galdós displays that very acute sense of the difference between appearance and reality on which irony so frequently depends.

To conclude: *Fortunata y Jacinta* cannot in my opinion be called a tragic work, as Zahareas maintains, though it touches tragic emotions at times. Nor is it as superficial, over-optimistic or complacent as has been suggested. It has, rather, a depth of feeling for the ironic twists of existence which does not exclude a certain zest for life and an underlying confidence in gradual progress. Its four volumes, while not giving us a full sociological conspectus of society, are thoroughly immersed in the political, social, economic and environmental reality of the Madrid of the 1870s. The portrayal of both individuals and the society they inhabit is artistically plausible and coherent in its detail and precision. Its language and its narrative technique have the subtlety required to present effectively the complexities of human behaviour, and especially the ambiguities of moral conduct, within an essentially clear and simple structure. Some minor deficiences have been noted. The novel is over-extended in parts; on occasions the narration is too explicit, and it may be that too confident a tone is adopted about the laws of society and the intermingling of classes. I hope nonetheless that what has been said about its qualities in these pages will persuade anyone not already convinced that *Fortunata y Jacinta* is one of the masterpieces of the European realist novel.

Bibliographical Note

It is impossible, within the scope of this note, to give more than a selection of the vast bibliography. For further references, see Theodore A. Sackett, *Pérez Galdós: an annotated bibliography* (Albuquerque, 1968), Hensley C. Woodbridge, *Benito Pérez Galdós: a selective annotated bibliography* (Metuchen, New Jersey, 1975) and the annual bibliography by Manuel Suárez Hernández in *Anales Galdosianos* (Austin, Texas = *AG*).

J. E. Varey's "Galdós in the Light of Recent Criticism", in *Galdós Studies*, ed. J. E. Varey (London, 1970), pp. 1-35, provides useful guidance.

HISTORICAL BACKGROUND
1. Raymond Carr, *Spain: 1808-1939* (Oxford, 1966). Standard work on nineteenth-century history.
2. Hans Hinterhäuser, *Los 'Episodios nacionales' de Benito Pérez Galdós* (Madrid, 1963). An excellent account of Galdós's use of historical material.
3. A. Regalado García, *Benito Pérez Galdós y la novela histórica española: 1868-1912* (Madrid, 1966). Less balanced than Hinterhäuser, it sees Galdós as a defender of the *status quo*. See the rectifications by R. Carr, *AG*, III (1968), 185-9, and P. Goldman, *AG*, VI (1971), 113-24.
4. Iris M. Zavala, *Ideología y política en la novela española del siglo XIX* (Salamanca, 1971). Useful description of rise of the novel, with anthology of theoretical statements. Includes Galdós's *Observaciones . . .* of 1870.
5. P. B. Goldman, "Galdós and the Politics of Conciliation", *AG*, IV (1969), 73-87.

BIOGRAPHY
6. H. Chonon Berkowitz, *Benito Pérez Galdós: Spanish liberal crusader* (Madison, 1948). Though dated and at times misleading, it remains indispensable.
7. Walter T. Pattison, *Benito Pérez Galdós*, Twayne World Authors Series, 341 (New York, 1975). A competent, though uninspired, study.

GENERAL CRITICAL WORKS
8. *The Age of Realism*, ed. F. W. J. Hemmings (Harmondsworth, 1974), has a section on Galdós by J. D. Rutherford, pp. 265-309.
9. Joaquín Casalduero, *Vida y obra de Galdós* (Madrid, 1951). A pioneer study, stimulating but marred by an excess of classifying zeal.
10. V. A. Chamberlin, "The *muletilla*: an important facet of Galdós' characterization technique", *Hispanic Review*, XXIX (1961), 296-309. A good account of a fundamental technical device.

11. Gustavo Correa, *El simbolismo religioso en las novelas de Pérez Galdós* (Madrid, 1962). An important study, somewhat rigid in approach.

12. Gustavo Correa, *Realidad, ficción y símbolo en las novelas de Pérez Galdós. Ensayo de estética realista* (Bogotá, 1967). Contains relevant sections on history and fiction.

13. Sherman H. Eoff, *The Novels of Pérez Galdós: the concept of life as dynamic process* (St Louis, 1954). Contains a thorough but rather abstract and jargon-ridden study of structure and psychology.

14. Ricardo Gullón, *Galdós, novelista moderno* (Madrid, 1960). Very wide-ranging, its usefulness is impaired by its over-ambitious scope. See review by G. Ribbans, *AG*, III (1968), 163-8.

15. Monroe Z. Hafter, "Ironic Reprise in Galdós' Novels", *Publications of the Modern Language Association*, LXXXVI (1961), 233-9. A highly significant study with wide structural implications.

16. J. F. Montesinos, *Galdós*, 3 vols (Madrid, 1968-72). A fundamental, though somewhat unsystematic, work of criticism. *Fortunata y Jacinta* is dealt with in vol. II, pp. 201-73.

17. Michael Nimetz, *Humor in Galdós. A study of the 'Novelas contemporáneas'* (New Haven and London, 1968). A significant study which contains, however, certain inconclusive arguments and dubious conclusions.

18. *Benito Pérez Galdós*, ed. D. M. Rogers (Madrid, 1973). A compilation of articles previously published, of little relevance to *Fortunata* except for Joseph Schraibman, "Los sueños en *Fortunata y Jacinta*", pp. 161-8 (see *21*), and Stephen Gilman, "La palabra hablada en *Fortunata y Jacinta*", pp. 293-315, reproduced from *Nueva Revista de Filología Hispánica*, XV (1961), 542-60.

19 Marie-Claire Petit, *Les Personnages féminins dans les romans de Benito Pérez Galdós* (Lyons, 1972). Includes interesting comments on the women characters of *Fortunata*.

20. A. Sánchez Barbudo, *Estudios sobre Galdós, Unamuno y Machado* (Madrid, 1968). Contains a useful study of "El estilo y la técnica de Galdós", pp. 21-45.

21. Joseph Schraibman, *Dreams in the Novels of Galdós* (New York, 1960). Factual rather than critical.

22. W. H. Shoemaker, *Estudios sobre Galdós* (Urbana, 1970). Contains an important study, "Galdós's Literary Creativity: D. José Ido del Sagrario", first published in *Hispanic Review*, XIX (1951), 204-37.

STUDIES OF 'FORTUNATA'
General

23. Sherman H. Eoff, "The Deification of Conscious Process", in *The Modern Spanish Novel* (New York, 1961), pp. 120-47. An influential study of the psychological and philosophical background.

24. Sherman H. Eoff, "The Treatment of Individual Personality in

Fortunata y Jacinta", *Hispanic Review*, XVII (1949), 269-89. An important article complementary to some extent to the last.

25.   P. Ortiz Armengol, "Vigencia de Fortunata", *Revista de Occidente*, 3ª época, nos 5-6 (1976), 43-51. A survey article by the most knowledgeable authority on the Madrid of Fortunata.

26.   S. Raphaël, "Un extraño viaje de novios", *AG*, III (1968), 35-49. A detailed examination of Juanito and Jacinta's honeymoon.

27.   A. Zahareas, "The Tragic Sense in *Fortunata y Jacinta*", *Symposium*, XIX (1965), 39-49; reproduced in Spanish in *AG*, III (1968), 25-34.

Narrative and structural technique

28.   K. Engler, "Notes on the Narrative Structure of *Fortunata y Jacinta*", *Symposium*, XXIV (1970), 111-27. A brief but perceptive study.

29.   Stephen Gilman, "Narrative Presentation in *Fortunata y Jacinta*", *Revista Hispánica Moderna*, XXIV (1968), 288-301.

30.   A. M. Gullón, "The Bird Motif and the Introductory Motif:structure in *Fortunata y Jacinta*", *AG*, IX (1974), 51-75. A symbolic interpretation which develops further Gilman's approach in *40*.

31.   Ricardo Gullón, *Técnicas de Galdós* (Madrid, 1970). Contains an important study, "Estructura y diseño en *Fortunata y Jacinta*", pp. 135-220.

32.   R. L. Utt, " 'El pájaro voló': observaciones sobre un leitmotif en *Fortunata y Jacinta*", *AG*, IX (1974), 37-50. Another continuation of Gilman's symbolic interpretation (see *40*).

Language

33.   G. A. and J. J. Alfieri, "El lenguaje familiar de Pérez Galdós", *Hispanófila*, no. 22 (1964), 27-73. Includes a useful list of colloquialisms in *Fortunata*.

34.   S. Bacarisse, "The Realism of Galdós: some reflections on language and the perception of reality", *Bulletin of Hispanic Studies*, XLII (1965), 239-50. A detailed stylistic examination of a passage from *Fortunata*: IV, vi, 13.

35.   James Whiston, "Language and Situation in Part I of *Fortunata y Jacinta*", *AG*, VII (1972), 79-91. A perceptive article which demonstrates the integration of language and structure in the novel.

See also *18*.

Society

36.   Carlos Blanco-Aguinaga, "On 'The Birth of Fortunata' ", *AG*, III (1968), 13-24. A socio-realist interpretation of the novel, emphatically refuting Gilman (see *40*).

37.   Geoffrey Ribbans, "Contemporary History in the Structure and Characterization of *Fortunata y Jacinta*", in *Galdós Studies*, ed. J. E. Varey (London, 1970), pp. 90-113.

38. Julio Rodríguez Puértolas, *Galdós: burguesía y revolución* (Madrid, 1975). Contains a vigorous article on *Fortunata*: "Anatomía de una sociedad burguesa", pp. 13-59.

39. J. H. Sinnigen, "Individual, Class and Society in *Fortunata y Jacinta*", in *Galdós Studies II*, ed. R. J. Weber (London, 1974), pp. 49-68. An on the whole competent account of the class structure portrayed in the novel.

Characters

(Fortunata)

40. Stephen Gilman, "The Birth of Fortunata", *AG*, I (1966), 71-83. A fascinating mythological view of the character of Fortunata in terms of bird imagery.

41. Stephen Gilman, "The Consciousness of Fortunata", *AG*, V (1970), 55-66. A continuation of the previous article.

(Maxi)

42. J. C. Ullman and G. H. Allison, "Galdós as Psychiatrist in *Fortunata y Jacinta*", *AG*, IX (1974), 7-36. Contains a psychiatric case-history of Maxi and other medical comments.

(Doña Guillermina)

43. L. V. Braun, "Galdós' Re-Creation of Ernestina Manuel de Villena as Guillermina Pacheco", *Hispanic Review*, XXXVIII (1970), 32-55. A careful account of the real-life model of Guillermina, which shows a rather simplified approach to literary creation.

44. J. L. Brooks, "The Character of Guillermina Pacheco in Galdós' Novel *Fortunata y Jacinta*", *Bulletin of Hispanic Studies*, XXXVIII (1961), 86-94. A lively article which takes an unfavourable view of Guillermina's sanctity.